"If ever there was a timely book that illumines racism, the role of religion legitimizing it, and how to undo its dehumanizing power, this is the book. Its pages brim with insights:

"Europeans saw themselves as the only group that had achieved real 'humanness, which led our European Founders to design our nation pretty much only for the (truly) human ones,' which logically excluded women and African slaves, and to a large extent poor, propertyless citizens. (To this very day we do not have a Supreme Court that in its interpretation of the Constitution, recognizes and boldly confronts racism in our criminal justice system.)

"The attitude of White European superiority / Black inferiority entrenched itself deeply into American Christian identity ('We are a White Christian nation') which led Christian pastors and their congregants to view slavery and then segregation as 'natural' and 'God's will.' Although there was, from the beginning, Black resistance to oppression, it was not until Dr. Martin Luther King Jr. and the Civil Rights Movement that significant societal reform began to happen. And need I say, the struggle goes on.

"There's a whole lot to explore in this amazing book. It may well change your life. I hope it sets you on fire to pitch your energies into the struggle."

—**Sister Helen Prejean**, author, *Dead Man Walking,*
The Death of Innocents, and *River of Fire*

"*Deconstructing Racism* offers a road map to disrupt the cycle of racism by upending the roots of racism embedded in America's institutions. Daring and bodacious, the book presents a parallel analysis of the American church as an institution embedded in racism and resistance. It unveils the defiant roots of racism and how past periods of resistance end with the manifestation of new forms of racism. The authors then skillfully present a path for institutions to deconstruct current structures in order to reconstruct a more equitable society."

—**Tammi Fleming**, senior associate,
The Annie E. Casey Foundation, Baltimore, MD

"This extraordinary work offers brilliant analysis, long-awaited solutions, and practical hands-on tools to fight racism. The authors give the readers a pinpointed, clear understanding of racism written by two seasoned practitioners. Joe and Barbara ensure you cannot put this book down as they fill the pages with their decades of wisdom, experience, and skill in an easy-to-understand format."

—**Willard Ashley**, senior pastor, Abundant Joy Community Church, Jersey City, NJ, and author, *New Rules for Radicals*

"In *Deconstructing Racism* Joe Barndt and Barbara Major focus on racism in the church, but also in every system in the United States. No matter what systems we are a part of or interact with in this country, we face the same structural realities. We are all the products of the same history. It is a history most of us are not taught and do not know. This is a book powerfully written and a story profoundly told. The authors have between them a lifetime of practical application that makes real what they teach. Read this book, whether you are a part of the church or not. You won't regret it."

—**David Billings**, author, *Deep Denial: The Persistence of White Supremacy in United States History and Life* (2016), and a core trainer with The People's Institute for Survival and Beyond

"My training as a sociologist led me to focus on the role of race and racism in our society. After years of reading and researching, I became involved with two organizations which for decades participated in organizing and training against racism. During the 1980s I became involved with Crossroads as a trainer and a member of its board. Rev. Joseph Barndt was the leader of this national organization and focused his work on helping Christian denominations, particularly the Lutheran church, to become active participants in challenging racism in the church and in society. During the same period, I also met leaders of the People's Institute for Survival and Beyond, a community anti-racist organization from New Orleans, Louisiana. These two allied organizations influenced each other in ways that strengthened their perspective and their work in anti-racism. I was privileged to meet Barbara Crain Major in many anti-racism training events where Rev. Joe Barndt and Barbara participated. As a sociologist and as an academic, I had a good theoretical understanding of racism as a systemic force in the United States, but my exposure to Joe and Barbara strengthened my understanding of the necessity of organizing to dismantle racism within our society's institutions. Moving from a purely academic perspective, I was transformed by my exposure to these trainers and organizers, and I also became an anti-racist trainer. I collaborated with colleagues in the church and later in higher education. I have read numerous books and essays on racism, but this coauthored book provides a grounded understanding on how to dismantle racism within institutions and develops concepts and paths to build a path toward an anti-racist society. After decades of work and organization, this book united two of the most gifted and consistent national experts in how to build a path toward a third reconstruction, one that will lead our society to a more just, equitable experience for all. The alchemy that comes from the joint organizing and theoretical work of Barbara and Joe will provide people of faith and those who long for a just society the steps and the path to the deconstruction of racism and the construction of an anti-racist society for future generations."

—Victor M. Rodriguez, professor emeritus, California State University, Long Beach, and anti-racist educator, trainer, and consultant

Deconstructing Racism

DECON STRUCT ING RACISM

A PATH TOWARD LASTING CHANGE

BARBARA CRAIN MAJOR AND
JOSEPH BARNDT

FORTRESS PRESS

MINNEAPOLIS

DECONSTRUCTING RACISM
A Path toward Lasting Change

Unless otherwise cited, the Scripture quotations are from New Revised Standard Version Bible, copyright © 1989 National Council of the Churches of
Christ in the United States of America. Used by permission. All rights reserved
worldwide.

Cover design: Laurie Ingram Art + Design.com

Print ISBN: 978-1-5064-7011-5
eBook ISBN: 978-1-5064-7012-2

CONTENTS

PREFACE

During the past forty years, the two of us have worked together in community-based and church-based settings. We have listened to, learned, taught, and applied the systemic analysis that is the basis for this book. This analysis has carried us, along with many other people, to a far deeper understanding of racism. We have seen the difference it has made for community organizers and community and institutional members when exposed to an analysis of racist systemic power. Responses to this analysis have consistently resulted in comments such as

"I now know I am not crazy."
"This analysis gives words to my reality."
"You have changed my life."

These are profound statements about what happens when truth is brought to light. We have observed how an anti-racist power analysis has impacted hundreds of thousands of organizers across this country. We see the impact in the streets, in organizations, and in institutions, including those who represent such organizing efforts as Black Lives Matter, the Poor People's Campaign, and other forms of anti-racist organizing. A renewed dynamic energy is afoot and aimed squarely at bringing down systemic racism. Along with the Reverend William Barber, leader of the Poor People's Campaign and author of *The Third Reconstruction*, we believe that our nation is entering a new Reconstruction era. God is giving us another chance to get it right.

In *Deconstructing Racism: A Path toward Lasting Change*, we propose to address the need for the *systemic deconstruction* of racism, which we believe has been a missing link in previous "reconstruction" efforts. We argue that before we can reconstruct an anti-racist society, we must deconstruct the roots of racism that are embedded in all our nation's systems and institutions.

At the same time, as the Third Reconstruction approaches, we are readying ourselves for racism's counterattack. We have seen, for example, that a systemic analysis of racism scares the hell out of white folks. The negative reaction to *critical race theory* is a clear example of the anxiety, resentment, and pushback that are caused by a call to acknowledge and address racism through a systemic lens. In *Deconstructing Racism*, we unmask the trickery of systemic racism and the invisible pattern that keeps racism in place.

We are clear that there is no quick fix. This nation did not get to where it is overnight, and we will not deconstruct racism overnight. However, we know more about racism than ever before. Racism can be deconstructed and undone. The struggle for racial justice is a multigenerational struggle. We didn't start the struggle, and we probably will not be around to see racial justice come to fruition. But this struggle requires the commitment of our energies, hearts, and souls to believe and to work as if racial justice will happen in our lifetimes. Many of us have been socialized to believe that racism will never go away. We counter that belief with the assertion that racism going away is not racism's choice; we will deconstruct it and make it go away. *Deconstructing Racism* identifies and addresses the deeply rooted race-based identity, history, and culture within systems that must be deconstructed before or during the process of reconstruction.

Who We Are

Before progressing to chapter 1, we want to introduce ourselves, along with providing a few remarks about how the book is constructed.

BARBARA MAJOR: It is a pleasure to introduce myself to you. I bring to this writing partnership my experience of more than forty years of anti-racism training and organizing. I bring my eldership and my love, my passion, and my commitment to the survival and growth of my community. I bring the love of a mother for her Black sons and grandson. I bring my acceptance of the responsibility of being my family's matriarch. I bring the love that comes with the names I proudly answer to in my community: Auntie, Ma, Miss B, and Mrs. Barbara.

In my professional life, I bring a bachelor of arts in sociology and a master's degree in social work from Southern University in New Orleans. I bring more than forty years as a core trainer with the People's Institute for Survival and Beyond, the national anti-racist training and organizing institute. I bring respect for the inherent and profound wisdom of my community. I bring the knowledge gained from ten years as executive director of the St. Thomas Health Clinic, the first clinic in the country to proclaim racism boldly and publicly as the number one health risk in the African American community. I bring my belief that this nation will change. I bring the belief that organizing to undo racism is living out my life's purpose.

JOSEPH BARNDT: I am excited to bring to this writing partnership my experience of more than forty years of anti-racism training and organizing. As a Lutheran pastor, I bring a passion to help lead and push the church toward becoming the anti-racist church that I believe God calls us to be. I bring my willingness to believe in the leadership of people of color, and especially my belief that when Black leaders and other leaders of color said to me many years ago, "Go home and free your own people," I was not being kicked out of their community, but rather I was being sent on a sacred mission to my white community. I have come to understand that we who have become known as white people are victims of our own misdoings, imprisoned by our own racism, and in danger of losing our own souls.

Over the past years, I have been a congregational pastor, a community organizer, an institutional organizer, a teacher/trainer, and an author. For eighteen years, I was the director of Crossroads Ministry, a sister anti-racism organization of the People's Institute for Survival and Beyond. After that, I served for twenty more years as a core organizer/trainer with the People's Institute. Other books that I have

had the honor of authoring are listed in the bibliography at the end
of this book.

How the Book Is Constructed

We understand that readers of this book will be coming from many
different places on the anti-racism journey. We hope the book com-
municates with you in a way that helps you find yourself in a new
place in which we together can find a common meeting point. We
pray that the readers of the book will conclude, "Damn, I get it!"
and, if not already members, that they will join the movement for a
racially just society.

We have approached the content of this book using two different but related contexts. Chapters 1, 3, and 5 speak generally about
all the systems of society. Chapters 2, 4, and 6 focus specifically on
the church. It is important to note that in focusing on the church
in chapters 2, 4, and 6, we do not assume that all readers are Christians or will be involved in church organizing. We needed to choose
one system as a model that can then be applied to any other system
in society. Since the church is Joseph's specialty, that was not a hard
decision to make. However, there are other reasons for choosing
the church:

- First, we believe racism is a spiritual sickness, and we
  need above all to hear and feel a spiritual word of healing.
  We all need the assurance of the old spiritual "There Is a
  Balm in Gilead."
- Second, an obvious contrast exists between where any
  system or institution is and where it needs to be. In the
  church, that contrast becomes a chasm. If we can undo
  racism in the church, we can undo racism anywhere.

The chapters that address racism in the church (2, 4, and 6) offer
sections in which readers can reflect on their personal experiences.
Look for dark shaded areas with the title "Reader's Reflection."

When you find them, decide whether to immediately explore the questions that are raised or come back to the reflections later.

Acknowledgments

BARBARA: Writing a book was never on my bucket list, or so I thought. Traveling across this country, and sometimes internationally, I have been graced by learning from the experiences, knowledge, and wisdom of so many. I have been blessed to be trusted and loved by extraordinary people who others might identify as ordinary. This book gradually became a way to say thank you to those people. First, I thank my mama, Bernice Harvey-Magee-Warner, who taught me unconditional love. Mother Ella Rose Crain, you gave me life. My aunts Lillie Dean Bell, Mary Lee Thomas, and Wilmus Gray were the strongest, most loving Black women I have ever known. These beautiful Black women are the ones who gave me my sense of worth and belonging and my authority to claim my authenticity and strength as a strong-willed Black woman. I thank my sons: Gentry Major, who would cook and make sure I would eat as I wrote, and Akeem Crain, the one I call my political savage. I thank God for you two every day. To my brothers and sisters and their families—Patricia Levy (Pat), Deborah Trepagnier (Deb), Lilly Crenshaw (Lil), Keith Jackson, E. L. Crain (Buck), Ronnie Cansler, Michael Cansler, and Terry Cansler—thanks for loving me, having my back, and making me laugh in the most difficult times, and thanks to all the rest of my great big family. I could never ever leave out Barbara Jackson and Brenda Griffin, my best friends, my teachers, and my partners in fun and crime. I am thankful for the organizations and the people who continue to include me in their work for racial justice, the St. Thomas Community, the St. Thomas Health Center, the People's Institute for Survival and Beyond, the Collaborative, and so many others. In the early years of my journey to becoming an anti-racist organizer and trainer, I had access to some of the greatest minds in the anti-racist movement, including Dr. James Norman Dunn, Ron Chisom, Rev. David

Billings, Dr. Michael Washington, Rev. Daniel Buford, John Morrin, Rev. Joseph Barndt, Ann Braden, and Rev. C. T. Vivian, just to name a few. I owe so much to so many. God, I wish I could list all their names; God, I wish I could remember all their names. I thank them.

In the process of writing this book with my coauthor, I realized two things: I will never write another book unless forced to, and I was supposed to be coauthoring this book with Joe Barndt. In sharing my learnings in the book, I learned more. This book for me is a way of shouting out to all of those who have gone before me in the struggle for racial justice, "Thank you! We have not stopped; we will not stop until the battle is won."

JOSEPH: I give my gratitude and thanks to all the staff and organizers and trainers of the People's Institute for Survival and Beyond, and especially to Ron Chisom and Barbara Major, who have been fierce mentors and gentle, loving friends from the very beginning. Thanks also to leaders of national, regional, and local churches who have risked much to gain much by becoming anti-racist churches. To uncountable colleagues who gave to me and everyone so much before joining the ancestors, including Tom Smith, Pamela Warrick Smith, Wolfram Kistner, Dumisani Kumalo, Lucius Walker, and those loving friends who still walk the earth with me (you know who you are). Above all, to my spouse, Susan, for her patient and always-present love.

1

WHAT WE HAVE LEARNED ABOUT RACISM

All men are created equal.

US Declaration of Independence, 1776

Any alien, being a free white person . . . may be admitted to become a Citizen of the United States.

US Congress Naturalization Act of 1790

In 1492, Christopher Columbus—a lost Italian sea captain who thought he was in India—docked his ship in the Bahamas and initiated a nearly three-hundred-year-long process of colonization and racialization that laid the foundation for the construction of a new nation, the United States of America. The Declaration of Independence, one of the primary documents upholding the new nation's foundation, proclaimed this principle: "We hold these truths to be self-evident, that all men are created equal."

At the very same time that these beautiful words were being written, three building blocks were being laid as cornerstones for the construction of the new nation. They proclaimed "self-evident truths" that contradicted the self-evident truth that all men are created equal. These three building blocks were

1. the appropriation by force and occupation of the land that now comprises the United States of America;

2. the genocidal slaughter and confining to reservations of millions of Indigenous people to whom this land once belonged; and

3. the importation of millions of enslaved Africans, on whose backs the economy and the economic system of this nation were built.

The "self-evident truth" espoused in the Declaration of Independence, "that all men are created equal," applied to a very select group of men. It did not apply to Indigenous people or enslaved Africans, nor to any other people of color, and obviously not to women of any race. "All men" in the Declaration of Independence referred exclusively to white Europeans and was based on the blatantly racist assumption that in 1776, white men were the only men in existence.

Fourteen years later, in 1790, the assumption that "all men" applied exclusively to "white men" was given formal and legal expression when the newly formed Congress of the United States of America, in fulfillment of the mandate of the recently ratified Constitution, passed the Naturalization Act of 1790, which stated that US citizenship would be exclusively limited to "free white men." The harsh reality is that the deepest, most profound and sacred principle upon which this nation is founded is the conscious and intentional ideology of white supremacy.

Over the centuries, there has been a long and ongoing struggle to challenge and change this undisguised racist principle. Battles have been won and lost, and the outcome is still not determined. Today, nearly one-fourth of the way through the twenty-first century, white supremacy continues to dominate and define the American way of life. The words of the Declaration of Independence really meant that all *white* men are created equal, and that meaning has not substantially changed. The supremacy of whiteness in America is still "a self-evident truth." The racist foundations of our nation are still intact.

The purpose of this book is to seek answers to two sets of questions:

+ First, why is change taking so long? Why has progress toward the ending of racism been so difficult, slow, and unfruitful?
+ Second, how do we finally get this done? What have we learned from past efforts to dismantle racism that can redirect us toward new approaches and swifter progress in building an anti-racist movement that will bring us, finally, to the end of racism?

The primary argument in this book is not only that the forces *of* racism are still wrong and strong but that the forces *opposing* racism are also strong, even with their deficiencies and insufficiencies. The antidote has often been as harmful as the original illness, the attempted cure sometimes worse than the disease. By acting in haste or settling for ineffective and easy solutions, we have tried to satisfy the hunger for freedom with the fast food of superficial change. We have yielded to the temptation to cut down the weeds of racism by the stem, leaving the roots alive to grow another season of racist plants. We have not been pulling up racism by the roots. In the language we will be introducing here, we have not been "deconstructing racism."

Reconstruction and Deconstruction

Why is it taking so long? How do we finally get it done? In pursuit of answers to these questions, this book will focus on two interrelated concepts: "reconstruction" and "deconstruction." The concept of reconstruction originally came into being following the end of slavery in 1865 and described efforts to build a new way of life following emancipation. The Reconstruction era was a twelve-year period from 1865 to 1877, a time when exciting steps forward were taken to replace the system of slavery with a new understanding of freedom for all. Then tragically, in 1877, Reconstruction abruptly came to an end. It was followed by a post-Reconstruction era (1877–1954), a period of intensified racial oppression, when steps backward were taken to deepen and preserve racism. At the center was a vicious system of apartheid, often referred to as Jim Crow.

The Second Reconstruction / The Civil Rights Movement

Recently, it has become popular to borrow the language of Reconstruction, as it was used to describe the postslavery years, to examine another important moment in the struggle for racial justice— namely, the Civil Rights Movement, the turbulent fourteen-year period (1954–68) when racism was publicly and politically challenged.[*] As a way of emphasizing important parallels between these two historical periods, we will join with others in referring to the Civil Rights Movement as the Second Reconstruction era. By comparing and contrasting these two historic moments of Reconstruction, as well as the post-Reconstruction years that followed each of these two eras, we believe we can gain new perspectives on what makes effective change possible and sustainable.

A Coming Third Reconstruction

Finally, we will be using the term *reconstruction* in a third way, to describe a new stage in the struggle for racial justice that we believe is coming and that we hope is close at hand. The name we will use for this coming stage of history is "the Third Reconstruction era."[†]

---

[*] Our calculation of the length of the Civil Rights Movement is a bit arbitrary. We count it as lasting fourteen years, beginning in 1954 and ending in 1968. Its beginning in 1954 is commonly accepted, with the landmark Supreme Court ruling of *Brown v. Board of Education.* However, the end is more commonly associated with the 1973 occupation by the American Indian Movement of Wounded Knee on the Pine Ridge Reservation in South Dakota, which would make the Civil Rights Movement nineteen years in length. We have chosen, for reasons that will become obvious, to mark the 1968 assassination of Rev. Martin Luther King Jr. as the earthshaking event that announced the Civil Rights Movement's end, with all that happened between 1968 and 1973 classified as aftershocks.

[†] For this term, we give credit to the Reverend Dr. William J. Barber II and his book with Jonathan Wilson-Hartgrove, *The Third Reconstruction: How a Moral Movement*

Our goal is to prepare for this coming Third Reconstruction era by learning what went well and what did not go well during the first two Reconstruction eras. While we will not pretend to predict the future or assign actual dates to this coming Third Reconstruction era, we do believe it is close enough at hand that we need to be urgently preparing for it. In the coming years, we may look back on this present moment and realize with hindsight that the Third Reconstruction era had already begun. Whether or not it has begun or there is time still to prepare, the burning question is, What needs to be done differently? What components need to be added or subtracted in order to make a third era of Reconstruction the moment in history when racism can be defeated?

Deconstruction: The Missing Link

With this question in mind, we want to introduce to this discussion a second image—namely, that of "deconstruction." We understand racism to be a systemic "construction" that needs to be "de-constructed" before a new anti-racist construct can be "re-constructed" in its place. We believe this crucial task of deconstruction was a missing link in the First Reconstruction era (1865–77) and was also missing in the Second Reconstruction era, the Civil Rights Movement (1954–68). The absence of deconstruction strategies helps explain the limitations and the impermanence of the changes that took place during both Reconstruction eras. Even more importantly, we believe that the carrying out of the task of deconstruction is critical to avoiding the mistakes of the first two Reconstruction eras and essential to preparing for the coming Third Reconstruction era.

We hope all of this will become clear as we move forward in the next chapters to a deeper explanation and exploration of deconstruction. As we dive further into the process of deconstruction, we

---

Is Overcoming the Politics of Division and Fear (Boston: Beacon, 2016). Barber ties this vision to the South Carolina–based Poor People's Campaign.

believe it will be apparent that the concept of race must be deconstructed. Simply put, our primary message will be this: *Before we can reconstruct, we need to deconstruct.*

First Things First: A Common Definition and Analysis of Racism

Before exploring deconstruction and reconstruction further, we have some other tasks to deal with in this first chapter. First and foremost, we want to explore what a shared, in-depth understanding of racism looks like, how it came to be in the first place, how it was constructed, and where it is still embedded in the structures of our society. Before engaging in a discussion about where we are going in the anti-racism movement, we need to share a common starting place. The rest of this first chapter will introduce preliminary questions that we need to hold in common so we can be on this path together.

In what follows, we will present a summary of what we believe should constitute a common definition and analysis of racism. We know that some of you have already been involved in anti-racist organizing, while others may be coming to this conversation for the first time. We want all to come and take a seat at the table, but if this conversation is new to you, we have listed several "Racism/Anti-Racism 101" books in the bibliography to provide helpful background reading. In addition, at several places in the following chapters, we will refer to anti-racism training organizations that provide workshops designed to help individuals and groups develop a common analysis of systemic racism.

The Authority and the Experience of People of Color

Why is a shared understanding of racism and its conscious/intentional construction important? We can say from experience that one sure way to keep racism in place is to maintain confusion over what racism is, or better still, to allow those who benefit from racism to define what racism is. Historically, many popular and commonly accepted definitions of racism have come from white people, definitions that are distorted and dead wrong. A true definition, understanding, and analysis of racism must be derived from the experience of people of color. That means that on this writing team, it is Barbara who speaks and needs to be heard regarding the African American experience in this country. In this society, many mistakenly believe that white people can have empathy with Black people and can therefore speak for them. Empathy is the ability to share and feel what someone else feels. We believe that white people can sympathize, meaning they may possess a sensitivity or have compassion for an individual or situation, but that is not empathy. White people can never feel what Black people feel when it comes to living under racism. Of course, white people can certainly feel anger and disgust for what happens to another human being because of racism. When a white person decries injustice perpetrated against a Black person, many mistakenly read this outcry as evidence that the white person now knows what racism feels like to Black people.

Barbara Speaks

Only people of color have the ability and experience to articulate what it means to constantly have your humanity assaulted by racism. To write about racism is difficult; to live with it and have all the systems constantly reminding you that this nation does not recognize your humanity is much more difficult. As an African American, racism is in the air that I breathe and imposes itself on every aspect of my life. I can't run from it, and I can't hide from it. My only sane choice is to resist it and work to eliminate it. Thus, the definition and analysis of racism in this book are unapologetically proposed by African Americans. Through their resistance and resilience to racism, people of color have demonstrated their ability to survive and provide leadership to the anti-racist movement.

There is a very important place for white people in this movement. White people can be authentic partners in this struggle when they accept the leadership of people of color, who themselves have an analysis of systemic racism and are accountable to the communities they claim to represent.

An Ocean, Not a Puddle

Our previous understanding of racism had us thinking about it like a puddle of water. We knew it was a big puddle, not easy to walk through or around, but most of us had no idea of what we were up against. Now we know that racism is an ocean, and putting on a pair of rain boots and trying to walk across it or wade through it will just get you drowned. Let us take a deep dive into this ocean called racism and see what we find. From the perspective of people of color, racism is deep and it's cold. Racism is much deeper than white people calling people of color offensive names or vice versa. We know that getting along and loving one another will not change the outcomes for people of color in the systems of this society. We might see lots of loving interactions, and yet we also continue to see white people disproportionately benefiting from these same systems. We are not dismissing the importance of love but rather demanding that love include the deconstruction of these racist societal systems and institutions.

A Common Analysis of Racism

What is your definition of *racism?* The starting point for any conversation about race and racism must begin with this question. *Racism* cannot mean anything you want it to mean. *Racism* is not just another word for *prejudice* or *bigotry*. *Racism* cannot be defined by doing a survey of popular beliefs. A conversation about racism must be based on a shared common analysis, and the source of that analysis must be done by the communities that suffer because of racism.

Racism means different things to different people. Having many definitions of *racism* is no accident; it keeps us from working together. Therefore, we need to follow a path toward seeking a shared, in-depth understanding of what racism is, how it came to be in the first place, how it was constructed, and where it is embedded in the structures of our society. Here's the definition of *racism* we propose to use throughout this book:

Racial prejudice

+

Systemic and institutionalized power

=

Racism

A simplified version of this definition ("*Prejudice + Power*") was first proposed by Patricia Bidol-Padva in 1970 in her book *Developing New Perspectives on Race*. This definition represented the beginnings of an anti-racism analysis that moved the narrative beyond the individualized understanding of racism that had been the foundation for much of the work during the Civil Rights Movement. The People's Institute for Survival and Beyond added the word *race* to the equation and introduced the training process of defining each word of the equation for clarity. Since then, this has become the definition employed by many, if not most, anti-racism educators and organizers.

The analytical lens, based on this definition, would contain minimally four basic components:

1. The myth and illusion of race
2. Systemic power at the center
3. Internalized racial oppression
4. Anti-racist organizing for community and institutional transformation

Let's take a brief look at each of these.

1. The Myth and Illusion of Race

The first component of a unifying analysis of racism is a common understanding of the myth and illusion of race. Most of us in this nation have been socialized to believe that people have always been identified by their race. In fact, race did not become a designation for distinguishing between groups of people until the seventeenth and eighteenth centuries. Until that time, it was acceptable to distinguish people by nationality, class, or religion, but not by race. When we dive as deep as we must into this history, we will better understand how racism is perpetuated and have a greater appreciation for those who resist and survive it. Once this deep dive takes place, then we will also have the capacity to comprehend what is really being said when people of color say, "Racism is deep and it's cold," and we will add, "And it is not that damn old."

The idea of race and the accompanying racism we experience today is primarily a heinous concoction from Europe that arose during the seventeenth century, a time in Europe that was called the Age of Enlightenment. During this period, scientists were struggling to assert themselves as legitimate sources of knowledge and authority. Europe was also in the midst of aggressive colonialism and human enslavement. This period in Europe's history provided the fertile soil in which was grown the erroneous idea that some humans are less human than others. This invented idea of race complimented the false European notion of its superiority. This notion led Europeans who would later be designated as white to believe that they had the God-given right to colonize and enslave other human beings. The scientists who initiated the concept of race also developed a pseudoscience that gave the concept of race legitimacy.

Three primary inventors and promoters of the concept of race were Carl Linnaeus (1707–88), Johann Friedrich Blumenbach (1752–1840), and Georges-Louis Leclerc Comte de Buffon (1707–88).* These men were not the only race constructionists,

---

* See the bibliography for suggested readings related to these figures.

and we are not suggesting that the construct of race is all their fault. But let's just say that their theories had great influence. To this day, there are those who are still trying to prove that race is real and that the white race is the superior race.

The order of superiority of the races placed the Caucasoid race (Caucasian/European) on top and the Negroid race (Black people/ African) on the bottom, with other race groupings occupying the space in between. Distinctions between the races were based on alleged differences in brain size and mental capacity, multiplied by other characteristics that uniquely qualified "Caucasian" as the only title for those who are fully human. When these designations completed the transition to identification by colors, the human ones were identified by the color white. All the while, the American colonies, and later the American nation, were built exclusively for the human ones, and white supremacy became the underlying principle that gave purpose to racial designations.

TThe following definition of race that we utilize has been developed from the work of Dr. Maulana Karenga, professor of Africana studies at California State, Long Beach, and further developed by Dr. Michael Washington, professor of African American history at Northern Kentucky University, Cincinnati, Ohio, and Barbara Major of the People's Institute for Survival and Beyond:

> Race is a specious (false and deceptive) classification of human beings, created by Europeans (who later became white) during the time of worldwide colonial expansion, to assign human worth and social status, using themselves as the model of humanity and the height of human achievement for the purpose of establishing, legitimizing, and maintaining white skin privileges and power.

This definition comes from Black people and is based on their lived reality. The belief in the fallacy of race is a foundational cornerstone of this nation's identity, history, and culture, ensuring that race-based identity, race-based history, and race-based culture will support the exclusivity and superiority of whiteness. Given the destructive impact of race on Black people, it is no wonder they feel that race and racism were created for the sole purpose of their destruction. However, the creation of race in Europe and its continued evolution in the United States had more to do with the stealing of resources and the enslavement of people for wealth and power than solely the destruction of people of color. This does not minimize the fact that people of color shoulder the overwhelmingly harsh and inhumane burdens of racism.

Race is not real, but racism *is* real. We have been socialized to believe that there is validity in our imposed racial identity. That simply is not true. Race was invented. At the same time, because the fallacy of race has been institutionalized, we cannot simply dismiss it. We are caught between a rock and hard place. It is only through the lens of race that we can identify the racial disparities within systems and institutions. When we attempt to address racism, the concept of race is often ignored or pushed to the background. However, it is race that is the linchpin for the proliferation of racism.

A central message of this book is this: So long as the concept of race is accepted as a classification of human beings, we can never create an anti-racist society. This nation must ultimately abolish the concept of race.

2. Systemic Power at the Center

A key to understanding racism is recognizing that racism is more than personal prejudice and individual bigotry. In this American society, the tendency is to believe that racism is only personal and individual and that changing one's heart is all that is necessary to become innocent of racism and to bring about its end. The confusion that prejudice and bigotry are the same as racism produces a woefully incomplete understanding of racism.

Racism is more than personal. It is systemic. The systems and institutions of society are structured in such a way that disproportionately favors white people over people of color—*automatically*! Let the definition of racism speak to you once more: *Racism = race prejudice + systemic and institutionalized power.* The distinctive mark of racism is power—collective, systemic, and societal power. Power can be defined in many ways. In a race construct, power is defined in terms of which racial grouping has the collective access to and control of all the systems and their institutions. The only people in this society who have collective access and collective control of all the systems are white people. In the early 1980s, Dr. Benjamin P. Bowser, Dr. Raymond G. Hunt, and others stated that "there are, after all, no significant formal institutions in American life—not the government, not the national economy, not the church and not education—that are not controlled by whites," and this remains true to this day.*

In the United States, *every system and institution was created originally and structured legally and intentionally to serve white people exclusively.* When systems were created in the United States, it was assumed that white people were the only people who had achieved full humanity. Native peoples, African Americans, Latinx, Asian Americans, and other minority people were not considered to be human. Systems and institutions were created for the real human ones; "all men are created equal" meant white men.

People of color know instinctively that no matter how bigoted an individual police officer, medical doctor, social worker, church member, salesperson, or elected official might be, it is the criminal justice *system*, the health care *system*, the social services *system*, the religion *system*, the corporate retail *system*, or the governmental *system* that is responsible for collectively perpetuating racial inequities and injustice.

A clear knowledge of what systemic power is must be the foundational pillar for a strategic plan to deconstruct it. By systemic power, we mean the legitimate/legal ability to access and/or control systems and institutions that are sanctioned by the state.

---

* Benjamin P. Bowser and Raymond G. Hunt, *Impacts of Racism on White Americans* (Newbury Park, CA: Sage, 1991), 247.

The institutions and organizations in a society are nearly as difficult to count as the stars in a galaxy. The purpose of these institutions and organizations is to create, produce, reproduce, manage, and distribute the resources of a society. A system is a collection of similar institutions that share common goals and purposes. Depending on which sociological school of thought you believe, there are as many as thirty classifiable primary systems in any given society. Each system is composed of thousands of subsystems—large and small institutions and organizations that share similar purposes and goals and function in ways that are interrelated, interconnected, and interdependent. Here is a list of the predominant systems in our society:

+ The *economic system* includes banks, savings-and-loan offices, and financial investment markets, and yes, it also includes all those payday loan offices and pawnshops in communities in which regular banking is not an option for some.
+ The *political system* consists of every governmental office, agency, legislative unit, and judiciary and the process for selecting political representation.
+ The *religious system* includes every church, temple, synagogue, mosque, and other religious institution or movement.
+ The *health care and medical system* includes doctors' offices, hospitals, clinics, pharmaceutical companies, drugstores, and research laboratories.
+ The *education system* is composed of numerous individual public and private schools, colleges, and universities.
+ The *communication and media system* is composed of a huge number of newspapers, books, radio and TV stations, magazines, internet networks, social networks, and related systems.

+ The *production and distribution system* brings food and clothing, electricity, tools, toys, and much more to our doorsteps.
+ The *criminal justice system* includes police departments, courts, jails, and prisons.
+ The *housing and real estate system* provides beds, offices, and meeting spaces for tonight's rest and tomorrow's work.
+ The *social services system* seeks protection for vulnerable children, the elderly, and many in between.
+ The *military system* includes armed forces to protect the resources, people, and systems of a society.
+ The *transportation system* is made up of roads, bridges, and all the different modes of transport.

Each of these systems is made up of hundreds of thousands of large and small institutions and organizations. Systems are relatively free-flowing and function with limited regulation and enforcement, in contrast to institutions and organizations that compose a system and are regulated by complex principles and laws. Changes in institutions and organizations are closely monitored and regulated, while systemic change is only measurable as the long-term product of institutional changes. Every successful step of institutional change brings a system closer to the tipping point of systemic transformation. Except in times of revolution, change in issues of societal justice, including racial justice, happens incrementally. Regarding racial justice and other forms of societal justice, we are today building on the efforts of those who struggled before us. We are mightily grateful to those who in the past challenged this nation on its lack of racial justice. We believe that these sheroes, heroes, and nonbinary warriors bought us some time, many with their lives. The time bought has allowed us to become clearer about what we are up against.

3. Internalized Racial Oppression

The third component of a shared analysis of racism is internalized racial oppression (IRO), and it includes two parallel concepts: *internalized racial inferiority* (IRI) and its application to people of color and *internalized racial superiority* (IRS) and its application to white people.

The concept of internalized racial oppression is a relatively recent addition to our analysis of racism, and we are discovering more about it every day. The one thing to keep in mind during the following discussion is that the concept of race is not real, and therefore the process of internalization is about how we learn to accept an illusion in our lives as though it were real.

What is internalized racial oppression? The internalization of racial oppression refers to the process of consciously and subconsciously accepting and acting out our assigned racial roles in a racially constructed society. When we are born, we are assigned our individual racial identity as well as our collective racial group. For example, Barbara was assigned the racial identity of African American or Black and in addition was assigned to be part of the racial group known as "African American." Joseph was assigned the individual racial identity of "white person" and is therefore part of the white racial collective. Immediately upon receiving our assigned individual and collective racial identities, the process of internalization began. We are socialized to feel a sense of belonging, to accept our assigned roles in the racial hierarchy, and to live and act them out, both consciously and subconsciously. And we learn to be uncomfortable with and to feel tension and mistrust toward other racial groupings. This internalization of racial oppression invades the deepest part of a human being and imprisons the very soul of a person. When the internalization of racial oppression is complete, we no longer can choose for ourselves who we are, who we belong to, or why we are even here. We fall in line and do what is expected of us as a member of our assigned race, with people of color accepting and acting out internalized racial inferiority and white people accepting and acting out internalized racial superiority.

Barbara's Reflections on Internalized Racial Inferiority

Internalized racial inferiority is defined as a complex multigenerational socialization process in which people of color take in and live out an assigned racial identity, one rooted in a race construct that has labeled our races as inferior. This process is legitimized, supported, and perpetuated through every system in this society. More of our behaviors than we realize are rooted in the acceptance of our inferiority and of our positions on the racial identity ladder—with white at the top, Black on the bottom, and all other races in between.

What makes IRI even more complex is that some of the manifestations of the internalization of inferiority become necessary for our survival. For example, we maintain silence when we are being harassed illegally and violently by the criminal justice system. We accept the abuse and question the motivation and methods of those who challenge the abuse. We internalize our inferiority when we allow racist abuse to go unchallenged. We develop coping skills and pass them on to the next generation. The internalization of these abuses impacts our psychic and physical health, our spiritual being, and our self-esteem. However, mastery of these coping skills is required in this society for our safety and survival.

The internalization of inferiority is manifested in many ways. I will only highlight five of those that support and maintain the race construct.

- **Worthlessness.** The feeling that we are "worth less" compared to other human beings. When we believe and act out our feelings of worthlessness, we feel like we must add clothes, cars, houses, and other material things to give us worth. The material things owned by someone who looks like us are more valued than that person's life. For some of our young people, this translates to "You look like me, but I ain't worth nothing, so you ain't worth nothing; only your stuff is worth something. I'll take your stuff and your life."

- Colorism. We treat one another based on the color variations of our skin, believing that the closer we can get to being white, the closer we get to the highest standard of humanity and beauty. The whiter you are, the more human and beautiful you are. We have internalized this racist standard of beauty and apply it to one another. Our babies continue to be battered with this false belief in what is good and beautiful.

- Rage. Anger can turn into uncontrolled rage. The unacknowledged legitimacy of our anger is the result of the constant abuse of racism and results in the inability to give ourselves the right to be angry. We understand that expressing anger has negative consequences and is most often detrimental to our existence, so we are forced to keep it inside or regurgitate it on those who look like us. When allowed to fester, this anger often turns into rage, which can make us physically ill and keeps us in a perpetual state of spiritual and mental torment. Unacknowledged, this anger will either implode or explode.

- "Crabs in a barrel." Too often we criticize our people for acting like crabs in a barrel, by tearing one another down. My colleague Dr. Kimberley Richards often asks, "Who built the barrel and put us there? The barrel is not a natural habitat for a crab." We've internalized the belief that we are somehow worse at supporting one another than are other racialized groups. In fact, the opposite is true: our survival has always depended on our mutual support.

- Protecting the status quo. We defend and protect white supremacist individuals, institutions, and systems at the cost of our humanity, integrity, and spiritual connection with and relationship to the Black collective. When we are willing to sacrifice these things, we keep in place a system that does not see us as full human beings. This includes the inability or the unwillingness to acknowledge racist actions and positions taken by the organizations or institutions of which we are a part to maintain our assigned conditional position of power within that organization or institution.

Joseph's Reflections on Internalized Racial Superiority

Internalized racial superiority is a complex multigenerational socialization process in which white people live out an assigned racial identity rooted in a race construct that has assigned the white race as the superior race. This process is legitimized, supported, and perpetuated through every system in this society. Much of the behavior of white people is rooted in the acceptance of the belief in our superiority. These superior behaviors have defined and normalized the construct of white supremacy. IRS manifests itself in conscious and overt ways as well as in covert and subconscious ways. Because white supremacist behavior is normative, many white people find it difficult to recognize when we are subconsciously projecting white supremacy. However, African Americans and other people of color are extremely familiar with identifying when white superiority is being exercised.

Internalized racial superiority has many manifestations. As with IRI, I will only highlight five of these:

- White people are in control and in charge. It is white people's world. White people control resources, people, organizations, and institutions, and they believe that people of color do not have the experience or capability to occupy these white positions. This is not only the reactionary behavior of white people with consciously negative feelings toward people of color. It is an even greater problem with liberal, paternalistic white people who love people of color and feel the need to take care of them.

- The right to comfort and safety. The belief that white people must always feel safe and comfortable translates into the right to determine the place and position of people of color. This is particularly noticeable when engaged in a conversation about race. This need for comfort also manifests itself in the belief that white people should be trusted. In a multiracial setting, white people don't feel comfortable unless we are assured that people of color trust us.

- The experts on understanding people of color. White people, we believe we know everything about Black people and other people of color, seeing ourselves as saviors who have the right to go into Black communities and other communities of color to help/save them by means of their religion, programs, and policies.

- Individualism. This major tenet of American civil religion claims that I can do and have done it all by myself. Who needs the community? I can lift myself up by my own bootstraps. Freedom is measured by individual rights and not by the rights and needs of the larger collective.

- Entitlement. It's a white people's world, and we are entitled to discover it, claim it, colonize it, and do with it whatever we choose. This is the belief that white people have a right to everything they have or want.

Internalized racial oppression keeps us in separate worlds. White people, too, are prisoners of racism. We won't be able to stop being racists until race and racism no longer exist. White people cannot stop the automatic benefits they receive from being white. But our inability to recognize these manifestations will forever keep us from creating authentic relationships. Internalized behaviors did not happen overnight, and I (Barbara) recognize that, for me personally as an African American, these learned behaviors will require a lifetime to clean up. Also, the deeper question is not just how to correct these behaviors but how to prevent their development in the first place. That is the subject we will be dealing with in the following chapters when we enter the conversation about deconstructing racism.

This conversation is not about blame; it is a conversation about recognition. These two distorted identities of who we are feed and strengthen the white supremacist construct. There is no quick fix; it has taken multiple generations for us to get to this place. Before we can move forward to building an anti-racist society, we must acknowledge that there has been damage done to all of us. It will be easier for us to go where we want to go if we can identify where we are and how we got here.

4. Anti-racist Organizing for Community and Institutional Transformation

The fourth component of a shared analysis of racism is the task of organizing to end racism. It is extremely important to affirm that we are not hopelessly bound to racism. Racism can be ended. Racism can be stopped. Racism was done, and it can be undone. That which has been constructed can be deconstructed. This is not an unrealistic or whimsical wish or dream. Rather, it is an appraisal of the possibilities for change based on the history of resisting racism and the organizing that has taken place to move us to the place in history that we now occupy.

Every positive change for justice and human rights in this nation has happened, not because the nation naturally evolved into believing it was the right thing to do, but because people organized and fought for that change to happen. We believe that an organized anti-racism movement can uproot racism in the systems of this nation. The United States of America was constructed with the conscious and intentional ideology of racist white superiority, and we can consciously and intentionally deconstruct race and reconstruct anti-racism within every system in this nation.

We are not suggesting that the deconstruction of racism will be quick or easy. What we know is that we are following in the path of giants who accomplished so very much before our time. Standing on their shoulders, we should be able to stand taller and see farther. Attempts to dismantle and undo racism have been around as long as racism itself. The power of racism to control us has been enormous. It has even controlled the way we define it and the way we have gone about trying to undo it. Racism has controlled systemic change and set the limits on how much it would allow systems to change. Our organizing task is to deconstruct racism and radically reconstruct every system in this nation. Anti-racist organizing must be grounded in a clear understanding of systemic and institutionalized racism.

Barbara: For many years, I described myself as a community organizer, and in fact I was. Now I describe myself as an anti-racist community organizer. The difference is monumental. When I was not clear about racism, I was just spinning my wheels, attempting to fit my community into institutions that had not been created for them. As an anti-racist organizer, I now realize that my organizing must be aimed toward transforming these systems—structurally, conceptually, ideologically, and spiritually.

Transactional and Transformational Change

There are three additional concepts we want to mention before ending this introductory chapter. We will explore them in depth in later chapters, but it will be helpful to have them in our minds as we proceed. The first of these concepts is the distinction between transactional and transformational change. Transactional change relates to visible but superficial changes on the surface, while transformational change goes beneath the surface to bring about structural and foundational changes.

The deconstruction of racism and reconstruction of anti-racism depend not on our getting caught up with the superficiality of transactional change, but we're rather called to develop the capacity to bring about in-depth transformative change. Being satisfied with transactional change is almost a guarantee that the deconstruction of racism and anti-racist reconstruction will not take place. We have already witnessed through the example of the Declaration of Independence that no amount of transactional change will bring about transformation. And as we will see, nothing less than deconstruction will be sufficient to bring about transformational change.

Organizing Principles

The second concept we want to urge readers to keep in mind in coming chapters is the need for practical principles for organizing within communities and institutions to end racism. Working to transform systems and institutions requires both community organizing and institutional organizing. We have learned the necessity of agreeing to and employing anti-racist organizing principles. The organizing principles developed by the People's Institute for Survival and Beyond are, from our perspective, the most appropriate and make the most sense for community and institutional organizing. Take a few moments to read the following list of organizing principles. In the coming chapters, we will have the opportunity to explore most of these further. With a growing understanding and a strategic employment of these organizing principles, our deconstructing efforts will have visible and long-lasting impacts.

THE PEOPLE'S INSTITUTE FOR SURVIVAL AND BEYOND

Principles of Anti-racist Organizing™

To Build a Movement for Social Justice and Equity

Undoing Racism—We understand racism as a dehumanizing ideology that is the single most critical barrier to building effective coalitions for social change. Racism has been consciously and systematically constructed. It can be undone as people understand what it is, where it comes from, how it functions, and why it is perpetuated.

Understanding, Sharing, and Celebrating Culture—We recognize culture as a way of life—the life-support system of a community. When people understand, respect, and nurture their culture, they get a sense of their own power. In the United States, the dominant culture has been dehumanized by racism. Understanding this dominant culture is the first step toward transforming it into a humane culture.

Learning from History—We believe that history is a tool for effective organizing. History teaches that all institutions in the United States have roots that can be traced back or linked to periods of genocidal enslavement or separate-but-equal policies that have created inequities in wealth and access to and control of those institutions. As individuals and organizations research our history, we are able to use anti-racist principles to create a more just and equitable future.

Analyzing Manifestations of Racism—We identify manifestations of racism in *individuals, institutions, culture, language,* and our relationship to our *environment.* These forms of racism are interrelated. For example, individual racism is nurtured by the dominant culture and backed up by institutions. Racism manifested as *militarism* is enforced by police at home and armies abroad. In order to dismantle racism, we must analyze the power of its interlocking manifestations.

Networking—We recognize that the growth of a movement for social transformation requires networking— "building a net that works." Networking means building principled relationships based on humane values. These relationships, in turn, allow us to create alliances across issues and ideologies that otherwise tend to divide us. As the movement develops strong networks, people are less likely to fall through.

Undoing Internalized Racial Oppression—We understand that internalized racial oppression manifests itself both as *internalized racial inferiority* and as *internalized racial superiority*. It leads individuals, institutions, and whole systems to accept and act out definitions of individuals and groups that are rooted in a racial construct that designates one or more "races" as inferior and others as superior. Over many generations, *internalized racial inferiority* expresses itself in such self-defeating behaviors as self-blame, rage, colorism, ethnocentrism, denial, and so on. The process of *internalized racial superiority*, over generations, gives those designated as a "superior race" unearned privileges and unacknowledged power and often makes their racial advantages invisible to them. Naming and analyzing internalized racial oppression are the first steps in overcoming its debilitating effects.

Developing Leadership—We believe that anti-racist organizers need to be intentionally and systematically developed within local communities and organizations.

We especially encourage and mentor young people and grassroots leaders to find their voices and assume their rightful roles as anti-racist organizers.

Maintaining Accountability—We have learned that to organize with integrity requires that we be accountable to those communities that struggle with racism. Individuals and institutions that serve, work on behalf of, and obtain resources in the name of those communities must respect and follow their collective leadership.

Reshaping Gatekeeping—We recognize that persons who work in institutions often function as gatekeepers who ensure that the institution perpetuates itself. Gatekeepers who operate with anti-racist values and who maintain an accountable relationship with the community can help generate institutional transformation rather than perpetuate an unjust status quo.

These principles are trademarked by the People's Institute for Survival and Beyond.
Please use with permission and attribution only. See pisab.org for additional information.

Identifying and Naming the Three Primary Roots of Racism

Three roots of racism will be our target for deconstruction in the coming pages. The central message of this book is this: *So long as the concept of race is accepted as a classification of human beings, we can never create an anti-racist society.* This nation must ultimately go to the roots of racism in every social system and abolish the concept of race. In the following chapters, we will further explore this task and follow a path to the roots of racism, where the deconstruction must take place. Our starting place on this path is to identify these roots, give them names, study them to discover their strengths and vulnerabilities, and then develop a strategic organizing plan that will lead to their abolition.

We suggest that three primary root clusters of systemic racism are embedded in every system and institution:

+ *race-based identity* prescribing, describing, and dictating who we are;
+ *race-based history* prescribing, describing, and dictating who we have been; and
+ *race-based culture* prescribing, describing, and dictating who we are becoming.

The deconstruction of these roots is key to the dismantling of racism for the purpose of creating anti-racist systems. However, systemic change begins with institutional change. A system cannot become anti-racist if its institutions are not anti-racist. The practical path to the longer journey to systemic change is the shorter goal of anti-racist institutional and community organizing.

Systemic Root # 1: Race-Based Identity— the Illusion of "Who We Are"

We referred to the concept of race as "specious," something that seems to be true but is not. Race is an illusion, but it is an illusion that carries within itself the feeling of reality. Moreover, the idea of race carries with it the acceptance of a racial hierarchy of superior and inferior people. White people and people of color alike are socialized consciously and unconsciously to believe in their respective superiority and inferiority. The shaping and reshaping of our race-based identities are perpetuated, reinforced, and nourished through the intentional design of every system and institution. We have been socialized not to question how systems and institutions work or do not work.

As long as the concept of race is perpetuated and accepted as real, there will be systemic racism. Until the fallacy of race is deconstructed, along with the white supremacy that inevitably accompanies it, the reconstruction of an anti-racist nation will be impossible.

Systemic Root # 2: Race-Based History— the Illusion of "The Way We Were"

This nation has not only accepted the illusion of race as reality, but it has also perpetuated the illusion that its history of race and the impact of race on its history are accurate. The true history is a horror story of colonization, genocide, and enslavement. The history of our nation has been so sanitized and ingrained in our conscious and unconscious memory that many find facing the truth of this nation's history to be unimaginably agonizing. The truth is, the history of this nation's origin celebrates the enslavement of African people, the stealing of Indigenous people's land and resources, and the sanctioning of the belief of superior and inferior races. The founding documents of this nation eliminate, devalue, and dehumanize all but white men.

Every societal system in our nation (government, economy, education, health care, criminal justice, etc.) is built on the foundation of this distorted history. This whitewashing has contributed to the present-day inability of systems to be changed to serve everyone with equity. We will never achieve building an anti-racist nation until we can openly tell the unsanitized truth about who we were and are and how we got here. Then the beautiful stories that also must be told will serve their own purposes and not be needed as distractions or cover-ups.

Race-based history is the history of a lie. Until this nation's history is deconstructed and rewritten (reconstructed) from a perspective that does not celebrate white supremacy, and until the histories of white people and people of color are given the same weight, the reconstruction of an anti-racist nation is impossible.

Systemic Root # 3: Race-Based Culture—
the Illusion of "Equity and Shared Power"

Culture is how you join with others to view the world and your place in it. It is what we hold sacred and valuable as an expression of our collective way of life. A race-based culture is the racialization of a people by a dominant culture and the imposition of the dominant culture's worldview that has evolved from centuries-long viewing of reality through an unreal racial lens.

Race-based culture holds the abuse and subjugation of Black people and other people of color to be normal. The culture that emanated from a belief in the concept of race and racial hierarchy has been accepted as real and natural. After generations of this abnormal normal, we have internalized the lies of a race-based culture. Every system in this nation is rooted in a white supremacist worldview, and these systems have given birth to white institutions and white institutional culture. In a race-based culture, no other way of seeing and being in relationship with the world matters. Race-based culture values profit over people, individualism over collective interdependence, and hierarchy over equity. Deconstruction of a race-based culture is the dismantling of a dominant culture's systemic, institutionalized power.

Until this nation's racialized culture is deconstructed, along with the power of the dominant white race to impose its worldview on other cultures, the reconstruction of an anti-racist, multicultural nation cannot take place.

2

SYSTEMIC RACISM AND THE CHURCH

A Tale of Two Churches

> *They are endowed by their Creator . . .*
>
> US Declaration of Independence, 1776

As we indicated in the preface, the structure of this book is designed to focus every other chapter (chapters 1, 3, and 5) on how racism invades and controls all systemic structures of American society. The other chapters (chapters 2, 4, and 6) focus more deeply on one of those systems to provide a studied example of racism in a specific systemic setting. By focusing on one societal system, we will portray an example of how racism is systemically embedded in all systems of our society. Since it would require volumes to carry out this deeper exploration in every system, we have chosen the alternative approach of modeling an in-depth exploration of one of these systems—namely, the church. Hopefully this extended example will also provide a model for readers wanting to do similar in-depth exploration of other societal systems.

Why the Church?

We have chosen the system of religion, and particularly the institution of the Christian church, as a model to not only demonstrate how racism is embedded through a system but also show how it is possible to eliminate racism from societal systems. We could have chosen any one of the twenty or more primary societal systems (see pp. 14–15). Any societal system could serve as a model for reflecting on how racism is infused systemically in our society. From our perspective, we have chosen the system of religion and the specific institution of the Christian church for two primary reasons. First, racism is a deeply spiritual issue. Yes, it is also an economic, sociological, and psychological issue; all societal systems are engulfed by racism, and any one of them could be a starting point for a conversation about systemic racism. But we believe that at its very deepest, racism is a spiritual disease, a sickness of the spirit of a people, a relational condition that affects the stability of our common lives and our very ability to be in community. Starting with racism's spiritual dimensions means starting at the heart of the issue.

Second, how our nation responds to and seeks to solve the problem of racism is a mark and measure of our national spiritual strength and maturity. The United States defines itself as a religious nation. The will of God and the will of the nation have been intimately connected from the beginning of our history. Very few decisions were made by our nation's founders that did not include a reference to the importance of being obedient to the will of God. This role of religion in our nation's founding is clearly articulated in the Declaration of Independence, which states that the inalienable rights of citizens are "endowed by their Creator." This simple phrase, "endowed by their Creator," not only proclaims and affirms the profound role that religion played in the nation's founding. Even more importantly for our purposes, it points to how racism and divinely blessed white supremacy have been defined and ensured by this intimate relationship between church and state. We have already pointed out in chapter 1 that the founders of this nation in their composing the Declaration of Independence made no effort to hide their conviction that the category of "all men" refers only to white men and that only white men were the recipients of "certain inalienable rights, including among these being life, liberty, and the pursuit of happiness."

Looking back at our nation's creation story requires a difficult and painful confrontation with reality. We need to acknowledge and confess that the white supremacy in our nation's founding was not a fringe problem caused by a few bigoted individuals, but rather it was from the beginning a central ideological and theological principle upon which the foundations of our nation were designed and established. We need to repeat it again and again until we stop trying to deny it: the European colonists saw themselves as representatives of the only race that had achieved the status of humanness. In their eyes, no one other than Europeans and European Americans had been granted this coveted status. And it was in this same context of exclusive humanness that European American colonists proudly claimed, beginning around the year 1700, a new self-designation of "white people." From this position of human self-consciousness, they then proceeded to shape a nation designed exclusively for the human ones, for white people. Most importantly, at this moment in the twenty-first century, this exclusive consciousness has not fundamentally changed. In the ideological, structural, and cultural roots of our nation lies a self-perpetuating white supremacy that continues to dominate, define, and divide the American way of life. And that dividing line also cuts sharply into a racially divided Christian church. For that reason alone, it is important that an analysis of race and racism in America includes a focus on the role of the Christian church in both the construction and the deconstruction of racism.

A Racist Church

In the era of global colonization, the church of the European colonizers became the predominant religion wherever European colonies were established. European Christian denominations (Lutheran, Reformed, Methodist, Roman Catholic, Presbyterian, Methodist, Episcopalian, etc.) were transplanted to colonies everywhere as duplicates of their mother churches in Europe. This was especially true in the colonies in North America.

Thus, in this chapter, and in succeeding chapters 4 and 6, one of our primary goals is to explore how Christianity, contrary to its theoretical teaching of inclusivity, has had an indisputable record of repeatedly and shamelessly supporting racism, claiming divine authority to do so by twisting and distorting the Bible and the teachings of the Christian faith. A common denominator shared by nearly all these colonial churches was the exclusive whiteness of their membership and their willingness to serve as the official religion of the colony. As the nation gained independence, it defined itself constitutionally as existing exclusively for white people. The colonial churches became an integrative force for a white supremacist ideology and theology. They created moral and ethical norms consistent with white supremacy and helped maintain the social acceptance of slavery and Native genocide. As such, these predominantly white Protestant and Roman Catholic denominations became stabilizing pillars of colonial life and functioned in the role of a state church. With few exceptions, the churches were glad to be invited to play such an important role and responded with pledges of loyalty to the new nation.

Representatives of the white colonial churches also joined the pioneers in their covered wagons as the frontiers of the nation expanded westward, simultaneously blessing the appropriation of new land and the slaughter of Native peoples while also baptizing those who escaped the slaughter and helping assign them to reservations and to the lowest rungs of the societal (and Christian) ladder. It is very important to be open and honest about this. Only as we shine the light of truth on these shameful and disgraceful actions can we receive guidance on how to follow a path of healing that can lead toward true forgiveness and reconciliation.

An authentic healing process requires that before our churches can accompany the nation in addressing societal racism, we must simultaneously address our own racism within the church. Healing needs to be happening within the church if the church is to participate in bringing about healing elsewhere. This is not an easy task. Raising the issue of racism in the church inevitably results in defensive responses. It is difficult to admit that the sins of the world also afflict the church. It is especially difficult to hold that conversation publicly. Our first reaction is often to defend and protect the church. Nevertheless, we view the open discussion of racism within the church as a high priority, and we encourage Christians to look honestly at our history and the church's need for help in addressing racism. Especially because of this tendency toward defensiveness, we encourage that the initiative to deal with racism in the church be led by people who are part of the church and who love the church. We want to speak most directly to people who share a deep love for the church and who at the same time deeply feel the pain of the church's continued racism. Thus, we invite church people to embrace two tasks: first, to join the struggle to bring about change within the church; and second, to help the church become better equipped to be an instrument of God in shaping an anti-racist society.

The Other Face of the Church: Poor, Oppressed, and Anti-racist

There is another side to this story. When we shine the spotlight of racial identity on the Christian church in the United States, it divides itself into two separate groups: one consisting of denominations and congregations that are predominantly white, and the other consisting of congregations and denominations that are predominantly of color. While the predominantly white churches have a history of supporting racism, the churches that are made up of predominantly people of color have a history of challenging and condemning racism.

This second group of churches includes African American denominations such as the African Methodist Episcopal Church (AME), the African Methodist Episcopal Zion Church (AME Zion), the Church of God in Christ (COGIC), and a number of Black Baptist denominations such as the National Baptist Convention of America. The churches of color have heroically and courageously participated in the struggle to confront and dismantle racism. They have been joined in this struggle by Latinx churches that are mostly Roman Catholic and Pentecostal as well as Asian

American, Native American, and Arab American churches, some of which are separate denominations, but many of which are congregations of color within predominantly white denominations. Many of these churches of color, especially the Black churches, have unique histories of participation in movements to resist racism; this includes their leadership in the struggle to resist and end slavery, especially during the time of Jim Crow / legalized segregation, and their participation in the Civil Rights Movement. The participation of the Black churches in resistance movements has produced several well-known public leaders, including Dr. Martin Luther King Jr. and many others. Perhaps the most important image we have of these churches is their visible participation in movements to challenge racism at the height of protests in the 1960s, when the streets and the jails of our nation were filled with young people from Black churches showing their elders the path they needed to follow.

READER'S REFLECTION

If you are a member of a local Christian congregation, with which of the two groups does your congregation identify? Are you a predominantly white congregation, or a congregation predominantly of color? Does your congregation have a relationship with a church from the other group? Are you a church primarily of color in a predominantly white denomination? If so, is it a positive relationship? Do you worship together, or do missions work together?

- Read Ephesians 2:11–22. What images or phrases stand out for you? Why? How can this text be translated as a call to anti-racism? How does it help define or redefine your congregation's mission in a racially diverse community?
- Pray for the end of barriers that divide us.

Many white people are surprised to hear of the size of and power that has been exercised by churches of color. When, for example, the accomplishments of the Black church are described, a marvelously contrasting picture of the Christian church is revealed—one that proclaims a powerful message against racism. It is a message that has given millions of exploited and oppressed people hope and strength to survive and to participate boldly in the struggle for racism's elimination. Over the course of history, some of the most courageous and effective leaders in the struggle for racial justice have come from within churches of color. The strength, leadership, and determination of these prophets are witness to the power of the Christian faith.

Many denominations and congregations of color came into being in response to intolerable racism experienced by people of color in predominantly white churches. One well-known example is the story of the birth of the African Methodist Episcopal Church, which was formed in 1787 by Richard Allen, Absalom Jones, and others as a reaction to the racism of the white Methodist Episcopal Church. Forming separate denominations and congregations apart from the predominantly white churches gave them space to receive Christianity's message of freedom, comfort, and consolation in the face of racial oppression—a message they were not hearing in white churches.

We acknowledge that dividing churches into these two categories—predominantly white and racist and predominantly of color and anti-racist—has its limitations and does not tell the full story. The predominantly white Protestant and Roman Catholic churches have not been uniformly racist and have occasionally also been expressly anti-racist. In most white denominations, a visible and vocal minority has stood against the majority and sought to change the church. They have often identified with and supported the anti-racist stances of the churches of color.

Likewise, the churches of color have not been consistently anti-racist, and at times, these churches have shaped their identity by imitating the theology and culture of white churches. Nevertheless, in times of crisis around issues of race and racism, the predominantly white churches have stood with the white majority, while churches of color have identified with the resistance to racism, providing support, comfort, and courageous leadership for those racially oppressed.

READER'S REFLECTION

Barbara offers the following reflections about the Black church.

> As a Black person, I have had to learn to be conscious of the two faces of the Black church. Our internalization of racial oppression makes it tempting for us to condemn the entire Black church. Unfortunately, like many white churches, there are Black churches that believe services and programs are the answer to the racial oppression of Black people. Programs and services are needed, but to offer charity without a call for justice—I don't care who is providing it—is maintaining white supremacy. Many Black churches turned their backs on Dr. Martin Luther King Jr. during the Civil Rights Movement. But I also remember that Dr. King was a product of the Black church. The Black church is still a sanctuary for so many of my people, a place where their full humanity is acknowledged and a sacred liberating space for their spiritual connection to God. The Black church is and has been a foundational pillar for the survival of Black people. The church for many Black people is still the only place we can go for respite from racism.

+ How do Barbara's comments strike you? As you reflect on your experience of church, how have you seen racism perpetuated? How have you seen anti-racism at work?

Taking Racism Seriously

One of the main things that makes the situation in the churches difficult is the extent to which predominantly white denominations have pretended that racism is not real or that its reality is expressed only through individual prejudice and bigotry and not by the systemic design and function of the institutional church. Even more painful, when the white church has acknowledged the reality of the problem, they have often discounted its seriousness, believing that racism's negative effects on the church are superficial, that its permanent damage to the church is minimal, and that the problem can be solved without profound changes at the heart of the church.

We need to take racism in the church more seriously than ever before. This requires divesting ourselves of the defensiveness and denial that lead us into the temptation to cover up the tracks of our racism as fast as they are uncovered. Racism is a deadly disease. It is poison. It is the enemy that seeks to destroy us all, both white people and people of color. It is embedded systemically in the farthest reaches of our collective life, threatening to decimate the very soul of the church. Our goal in this book is to better understand the construct of systemic racism that has taken all our churches and each one of us prisoner and to develop the will and the skill to deconstruct racism and set our churches free. There isn't a chance in heaven or hell that we can do this until we are ready to go all the way to our foundations to bring about change.

Two Churches

So we have two churches: one is predominantly white, the other predominantly of color. And we have two stories to tell. One story is about the predominantly white church founded in racism and embedded in the myth of race and a fantasy of racial superiority. The other story is about a church with anti-racism branded into its foundations. Our task is to explore how the predominantly white church developed its racist systemic roots and to comprehend the source and location of the roots of systemic racism in the church. Then we can talk about the task of deconstructing those roots and reconstructing anti-racist roots.*

When the Christian church was born more than two thousand years ago, it was mostly a Middle Eastern and North African religion. Over the next fifteen hundred years, the geographic center of Christianity shifted from its Middle Eastern / North African starting place to Europe, with Rome as its capital. Christianity became a European religion and a powerful European church. Then during the next several centuries, beginning in the early 1500s, the influence of three major historical movements gave the Christian church its contemporary face and its racist roots. Let's take a brief look at these three events.

1. *The Reformation—a European Event*

The Protestant Reformation was principally a European event. Although it resulted in the fragmentation of the European church, it strengthened the identity of Christianity as a European religion. The total of all its pieces reflects the continuing centrality of the European church, adding only later the American church. Today, despite global expansion and the extensive growth of Christianity in South America, Asia, and Africa, the predominantly white Christian churches of Europe and North America still claim the principal role of defining the meaning and structure of the Christian faith. The hope is in the possibility that the next era of Reconstruction will permanently transform the church's power. But for the time being, the predominately white church of Europe and the United States is still in charge.

---

* For a longer and more detailed examination of the evolution of two churches—the Ruler's Church and the People's Church—from the time of their beginning in biblical times, see Joseph Barndt, "A Tale of Two Churches," in *Becoming an Anti-racist Church* (Minneapolis: Fortress, 2011), 27–35.

2. *The Age of Discovery—European Global Colonial Domination*

Beginning in the fifteenth century, Europe discovered and laid claim to ownership of the rest of the world. The result was global colonial domination. Inevitably, the European churches (including soon thereafter the churches of North America) claimed the position of God's representatives in the global colonial enterprise. Decolonizing movements of the past century have challenged much of European colonial domination, but the roots of global dominance run deep, and they carry with them the identity and alignment of European and North American Christianity.

3. *The Invention of Race and Racism*

Five hundred years ago, Europeans invented the myth of race. It provided a key element in creating the fairy-tale world in which Europeans named themselves the superior race of human beings, in contrast to the inferior, not-yet-fully-human beings who were being encountered in newly discovered lands all around the world. Although the concept of race was and still is a myth, out of the fantasy of race came the very real arrangement and practice of racism, adding the new and powerful weapons of oppression and subjugation to the arsenal of the colonizers.

In succeeding centuries, every aspect of life was impacted by race and racism. The Christian church was among the most deeply affected. The interpretation of the Bible and the church's theological foundations were shifted to make room for the idea of European supremacy. The church became a representative of colonialism, assisting in the dual tasks of building colonial outposts and the subjugation of those "not-yet-fully-humans" who stood in the way of the colonization process.

The representatives of the European churches accompanied and supported the colonizers, providing God's blessings on the establishment of a European-dominated world. In the process, the official

Christian denomination of a given colony was established, based on the predominant church denomination in the colonizing European country: the Anglican Church in the British colonies, the Reformed Church in the Dutch colonies, the Roman Catholic Church in the colonies of Spain and Portugal, the Lutheran Church in the German colonies, and so on. Thus, the colonial churches became racialized and became an instrument of extending racism's roots in every land and nation. The nearly five-hundred-year struggle between the colonizers and the colonized continues even today. Neither slave rebellions, Native American defiance, nor other forms of resistance have been able to fully eliminate the cruel racialization practiced by church and state. Thus, we point to the urgent need for a Third Reconstruction era and the hope it may bring for deconstructing the roots of racism in church and society.

Keeping Hope Alive in the Church of the Oppressed

Meanwhile, during the oppression of slavery, something unexpected happened among enslaved Africans and other subjugated and colonized peoples in the North American colonies. While listening to the missionaries teach and preach about the virtues of obedience, enslaved people began to hear another message that the missionaries did not intend to be heard. In readings from the Bible, they heard a message about freedom and equality that contradicted white people's claims of superiority, and they heard a message about justice that invited the poor and oppressed into a new relationship with God and with one another. It was there at the bottom of the white Christian ladder that a unique understanding of Christianity and of the Christian church came into being. At first, these contradictory messages lived quietly in the shadows, providing enslaved peoples the strength to survive and keeping hope alive in the hearts and souls of the oppressed. More importantly, the message of freedom and justice was preparing them for the life-and-death struggles that were yet to come. In the later days of the twentieth century, this new understanding of Christianity would be recognized as a precursor to the theology of liberation that we celebrate today.

READER'S REFLECTION

How has your church responded to the reality of racism? Was it with a willingness to address it? Or has it reacted by trying to cover it up with deflection and denial? Where do you find yourself personally on the path toward addressing racism in the church? As the book progresses, we hope you can discover new directions with us that contribute to the ultimate destruction of this old and powerful enemy.

Applying our analysis of the roots of the church's racism calls on us to face the church in its most ugly form and expression. This is a deeply personal conversation, and an embarrassing one that we often try to avoid. While racism is ugly everywhere, racism within the church is even more ugly than anywhere else. The standards and expectations of religion are usually very high. At its best, the role of religion in society is to provide moral and ethical leadership, to help the wider society focus on deeper concerns like meaning, purpose, values, ethics, and morality. At its worst, the church is a silent supporter of and participant in oppression and injustice.

Applying Our Analysis of Race and Racism in the Church

Let's turn now to the four-part analysis of the roots of racism introduced in chapter 1 and apply it to the context of the Christian church system. Recall that the analysis had the following four parts:

1. The Myth and Illusion of Race
2. Systemic Power at the Center
3. Internalized Racial Oppression
4. Anti-racist Organizing for Community and Institutional Transformation

1. The Myth and Illusion of Race

The church has been defined by the mythic concept of race, and as a result, its message and its life have been distorted. Race is not real. It is an illusion. And yet this myth has defined the church in many ways. For example, segregation is rooted in the church, though no church refers to segregation as part of its mission.

Race is a myth and an illusion, but racism is real. The reality of this statement should be especially clear to Christians, because the first issue of the Christian faith is one of identity. Christianity's first two identity questions are, Who are you? and Whose are you? When race is given the power to answer those questions, the segregated and superior white church is given a reason to exist.

Paralleling the myth of race is the lie of superiority. Buying into the illusion of race changes a person's fundamental sense of identity. The Christian world was structured on the premise of white people being superior, and the world was unnaturally divided, with the white and rich separated from poor people of color. There is no way to buy into the myth of race without simultaneously buying into the lie of white supremacy.

In the new nation of the United States of America, white people in the church, just like white people in the rest of the world, considered themselves to have achieved the full status of human beings. All others, especially enslaved Africans and Indigenous Native peoples in the Americas, had not achieved the status of "human" and could be dismissed and disposed of. Or they could become "objects of mission," targeted by the missionary enterprise, which placed them on the lowest rungs of the Christian ladder.

The churches of Europe blessed the colonization and racialization of the world. In the North American colonies, and later in the United States of America, the churches sanctioned slavery and supported segregation. Only with reluctance did the churches at the time of the Civil Rights Movement finally agree to integration. Still today, Christianity in the United States is racialized. There are a few multiracial congregations, but these are exceptions. Race is not a specter from the past; it haunts the church today. Race defines our borders, our membership, our culture, our theology, and our mission. It imprisons us and prevents us from truly being the church. Our beliefs, our worship, and our religious lifestyles are all racialized.

Deracializing the Bible

Even the Bible has been racialized. For centuries, the Bible was used to defend racism and slavery. Still today some argue that race and racism are based on the Bible's teachings. Understanding how the Bible has been wrongly racialized and used as a tool of racism is the most important first step in understanding and eliminating racism in the church. Of course, this means consistently stating, with billboard-style emphasis, that we accept responsibility for the race-based interpretation of the Bible.

Deracializing the Church

For most Christians, the scandalous reality remains that even if our daily life is increasingly multiracial, when the workweek is over and we head for church on Sunday morning, we are still walking through doors into congregations that are primarily red, brown, yellow, Black, or white. We remain largely locked away from one another, imprisoned in separate and segregated churches. Prison bars and gates are fitting images, in fact, for what keeps white people and people of color separated from one another, not only in our churches, but in virtually every aspect of our lives. Of course, it isn't difficult to see that racism places prison-like restrictions upon people of color. But white people are shocked to discover the imprisoning and destructive effects of racism in our lives too, and that all people are imprisoned by this evil power.

Those of us who are white are prisoners of our own racism. We have held the power of racism in our hands for so long that we are unable to let go. We receive power and privilege from racism, but in turn, racism gains power and control over us. Despite all the goodwill in our hearts, despite our deepest desires and intentions to become nonracists, we have been taken captive and are oppressed by our own racism. The imprisoner is imprisoned, and the victimizer is victimized. We are prisoners of the racist structures of our society, and there is no way the white church can be an effective participant in addressing racism elsewhere in society until we have found a way to effectively address racism in the church.

2. Systemic Power at the Center

The second part of our four-part analysis of racism in the church explores systemic racism and systemic power at the center. Here is the definition that we are using:

Race Prejudice in the Church

+

Systemic and Institutionalized Power in the Church

=

Racism in the Church

Racism is systemic. The primary assertion behind this definition is that racism in the church, like racism everywhere, must be seen as more than personal prejudice and individual bigotry. The reality is that in the predominantly white Protestant and Roman Catholic churches, racism as a systemic issue is avoided by perpetuating an understanding that racism is primarily personal prejudice and bigotry. Because of this, most white churches have difficulty going beyond building personal cross-racial relationships as an adequate response to racism. A church may think it is paying great attention to dealing with racism, but at the same time, it is avoiding addressing systemic racism.

As with all other societal systems, the Christian church was primarily founded by white people and was structured to serve its white members. The power at the core of the church was in the hands of white leaders. The church may have thought it was exempted from racism due to its spiritual nature and purpose. But like other institutions in our country, the church was created at a time when the white race was the only race that was considered to have achieved the full status of humanness, and therefore, the church was created to serve white people exclusively. Sounds crazy? We know now that it was truly crazy. But we didn't think so at the time.

Christianity's Racist Roots

Christian theological language can help us see how limiting it is to focus only on individual and personal racism and to avoid the profound impact of systemic racism. Christianity makes a distinction between individual sin and collective sin. A long-standing theological tension exists in the church between these two distinctly different dimensions of sin. It is a natural tension that should be complementary but is often expressed competitively. In the United States, where individualism is pervasive, the notion of collective, structural sin often seems foreign to us. We are willing to accept personal responsibility for our own individual sinfulness, but we frequently dismiss or deny our involvement in social and structural sins that benefit us but withhold benefits from others. Examples of individual sin include one person killing another, or stealing another person's property, or discriminating against another person because of class, race, or gender. On the other hand, illustrations of collective or structural sin would include the violence of war, the ravages of societal poverty, and systemic sexism and racism. From a biblical point of view, personal prejudice and institutionalized racism are both sins, but they are very different kinds of sins. Prejudice and bigotry are individual sins, while systemic and institutionalized racism is a collective sin.

> ## READER'S REFLECTION
>
> How does your church focus on "collective sin"? Are you aware of how racism and poverty are evident in your community? How does your church combat the collective causes of poverty and racism through teaching, preaching, and community ministry?

Racism Is a Collective Sin

When we apply these two theological dimensions of sin to the definition of racism, it should become clear that accepting responsibility for our sins of individual prejudice is not enough. We also need to be clear about the ways in which the white society acts together in collective or institutional ways to oppress people of color and to benefit collectively from that oppression. And we need to understand how to take collective responsibility for undoing what has been done.

Until recently, the Christian church has been willing to accept responsibility for the individual sins of prejudice and bigotry while strongly resisting taking responsibility for collective racism. Now, with that barrier beginning to fall and the language of systemic racism becoming increasingly acceptable, a new problem has arisen. Systemic language is being used to discuss racism, but individual racism is what is being primarily addressed. Using the language of systemic and institutionalized racism to describe individual prejudice and bigotry still hides the collective nature of racism. The result is a new layer of disguise that makes systemic racism yet more difficult to address.

Here is a clear definition: *Systemic racism is a collective sin committed on behalf of the white society and that provides benefits for all members of the white community.* A church that calls for a person to be free of prejudice but does not ask the same person to be accountable for collective racism is teaching and preaching only half of the Bible's understanding of sin.

To understand the power of systemic racism in the church and to develop an understanding of what it takes to challenge and bring about change, we must learn to perceive the sin of racism as it functions in the collective structures of society. Even more importantly, our awareness of systemic and institutionalized racism must include our awareness of its presence within the structures of the church. The church must take responsibility for the ways in which its own structures produce systemic results that benefit white people and fail to benefit people of color. Who holds power in the church? How are decisions made? Who benefits most from decisions that are made?

Power at the Center

Understanding systemic racism in the church requires us to take seriously the issue of power. *Racism = race prejudice + power*—that is, institutionalized systemic power. Such power is often misused to benefit those in power and disempower others. Christians tend to be very confused about power. We are not clear about what power is, whether it is good or evil, whether we like it or do not like it, or whether we should accept it or reject it.

From the point of view of the Bible and Christian theology, power is not in itself evil. In fact, quite the opposite is true. Power, from the point of view of Christian theology, is emphatically beautiful and good. Certain types of power can be a source of good. The Bible describes God's creative power in creation (Genesis 1) as good. Christianity claims that God wants humanity to receive and use power as something that is desirable and good. In the act of creation, God endows all people with potential power. In Jesus's last conversation with his disciples, he promises, "You will receive power when the Holy Spirit has come upon you" (Acts 1:8).

And the Gospel of John proclaims that "to all who received him, who believed in his name, he gave power to become children of God" (1:12).

What is power? Power is the ability or the capacity to become all that God intends us to be, individually and collectively. Power is not evil, nor is it neutral. Power is good. It can be wonderful, even delightful. Power is a defining human quality. We should want power and not feel bad about having it. We should also share power, thank God for it, and pray that we will use it for good purposes as it was intended and not misuse it for evil purposes.

The main point we want to make here is that although power is good, it can be misused. Whenever power is stripped from one group and overused by another, power is being misused. The Bible is very clear about the uncountable ways that God's good power has been greedily and violently misused when placed in human hands. Racism is power used for evil purposes. Racism is the misuse of God's good power.

3. Internalized Racial Oppression in the Church

The third component of our analysis of racism that we introduced in chapter 1 is the internalization of racial oppression. It is very important that we understand that the church's fundamental status as a racially segregated institution is an expression of the internalization of racism deeply buried in its roots. As described earlier, the invention of race and racism in the sixteenth and seventeenth centuries resulted in a racially segregated colonial church emerging as superior and the church of the colonized identified as inferior. The outcome was a rigidly segregated church, with the predominantly white Protestant and Roman Catholic churches of the United States manifesting characteristics of racial superiority (ownership, control, arrogance, paternalism, etc.) and the churches predominantly of color manifesting characteristics of inferiority (denial, acceptance of the superiority of the predominantly white church, etc.).

From this perspective, we believe it becomes clear why efforts to implement programs of multiracial/cultural diversity and inclusiveness have been consistently unsuccessful. Until the internalization of racial oppression in the institutional church is deconstructed in the church's roots, we will be frustrated by our failure to desegregate the church. Unless church programs, from birth to death, are designed to counteract the internalization of racial oppression, churches will continue to be instruments of racism.

To the extent that the church fails to reject and resist but rather accepts and encourages racial socialization, the church becomes an ally and instrument of racism. The tragic reality will continue to be that every time the church participates in assigning and nurturing a member's race, racism will be taking another prisoner. On the other hand, to the extent that the church understands the true evil nature of racism and recognizes the need to resist its own internalized racial oppression, the church then becomes the enemy of racism and a frontline instrument of God in the struggle for an anti-racist church and society.

From the moment a child is born, the church is offered the opportunity to participate in the deconstruction of the internalization process. Churches that practice child baptism or any other form of child dedication are equipped in a special way to participate in this early life struggle against racism. Racism, with its messages of internalized racial oppression, says to a child, "You belong to me." But in baptism, God responds to racism, saying, "No! This child is mine."

Listen to a question that is asked of parents and godparents during the baptism service: "Do you reject evil and all its empty promises?" Responding to this question "Yes, with the help of God" sets the stage for an ongoing, lifelong struggle between good and evil, between racism and anti-racism.

In the rite of baptism, there is also a "name-giving." At the same time we receive our "Christian name" in baptism, we also receive the name "Child of God, Resister of Evil," or even more specifically, "Child of God, Resister of Racism." Churches that encourage child dedication ceremonies communicate a similar message to that of baptism.

The point is that followers of the Christian faith from baptism on are called to resist evil in the world, and that includes joining the struggle against racism. The Bible and the historic Christian faith call the church and all Christians to take an uncompromising stand against the evil of racism and for the equality and unity of all humankind. Tragically, this is an underdeveloped potential in the predominantly white Roman Catholic and Protestant churches, and while churches and denominations of color do a better job than the white churches, their potential, too, is only partially developed.

READER'S REFLECTION

How can the church become more aware of the ways in which it supports racism and develop its potential for being a powerful instrument of anti-racism by countering the forces of internalized racial oppression? What keeps us from taking on this enormously important task?

The central question that we are seeking to ask in this book once again asserts itself: How deep do we need to dig in the church's foundations to bring us to the place where true transformation can take place?

4. Anti-racist Organizing in the Church

The fourth concept in our common analysis is organizing for institutional change. That which we wrote in the previous chapter about other institutions is especially true with the church—namely, that change doesn't happen easily or voluntarily. This is especially true with working for racial justice in the church. Past steps toward change have happened not because people's understanding naturally evolved in the right direction but because people effectively organized and fought for change to happen, moving the bulky weight of institutional bureaucracy in the right direction.

It is by far easier to recruit a few voices from a church to join with a few voices from other churches and institutions in the community to advocate for change outside the institution than it is to organize unified voices for change within the institution. It is possible to get a committee of two or three persons from the church to address an issue in the community, as long as the committee does not ask to speak for the entire church. On the other hand, if the organizing steps are reversed and the voice from the church represents the whole church, the power of that voice will be multiplied. If change is to be effective, that is what must be done.

We believe that an organized anti-racism movement can uproot racism in the churches of this nation. But because churches have been built on an ideology of racist white superiority, the task is difficult. Deconstructing racism in the church will take conscious and intentional action. We will address some of these specific actions in chapters 5 and 6.

Anti-racist organizing must be grounded in a clear understanding of systemic and institutionalized racism. The power of racism to control us has been enormous. It has even controlled the way we define it and the way we have gone about trying to undo it. Racism has controlled systemic change and set the limits on how much it would allow systems to change.

The anti-racism organizing principles of the People's Institute for Survival and Beyond, which were introduced in the previous chapter, are just as powerful and useful in church-based organizing.

Though all of this sounds like challenging bad news, there is good news also: churches of color have survived and kept their eyes on the prize. They have displayed profound understanding of the Christian church's mission of anti-racism. Though many predominantly white churches have not followed their calling to be anti-racist and some have openly supported racism, the purpose and direction of the whole church have not been lost. Those who are willing to follow the leadership of people of color will find renewed strength and, in the words of Saint Paul, "put on the whole armor of God" (Eph 6:11) and stand against the diabolical power of racism. The good news is the church can be restored as an anti-racist instrument of God.

READER'S REFLECTION

Who can you identify from your denomination, either in the distant past or in recent times, as someone who worked for peace and justice in our nation?

Whether reading this book sitting alone or as part of a study group in a congregation, university, or seminary, you are part of the much larger community of the family of God, a family to which we all belong. Perhaps you use traditional theological language to describe this community, such as "the communion of saints" or "the body of Christ." Or maybe your experience and orientation have taught you to add new and more contemporary expressions, describing your participation in "the movement" or "the struggle" or "the beloved community." These different expressions are not incompatible with traditional theological language but are complementary ways of seeing ourselves in the company of others, working for justice in the world.

Looking Racism in the Eye

Make no mistake about the seriousness of the task before us. To confront racism is to confront the diabolical presence of evil. To take on this enemy within the church and society is to take on a threatening killer that will resist elimination until its very dying moment. Yet only by recognizing the presence of this enemy in ourselves, in our churches, and in every part of society will we have a chance of overcoming this monster that will not easily be made to go away. It takes courage to stare this malicious enemy in its face. We need to pray fervently for the ability to overcome our fear of doing so. If we are going to take on the diabolical power of racism, we need a solid rock to stand on.

For our struggle is not against enemies of blood and flesh, but against the rulers, against the authorities, against the cosmic powers of this present darkness, against the spiritual forces of evil in the heavenly places. Therefore take up the whole armor of God, so that you may be able to withstand on that evil day, and having done everything, to stand firm. (Eph 6:12–13)

3

THE REPEATING PATTERN
OF RACISM AND RESISTANCE

Life, liberty, and the pursuit of happiness.

US Declaration of Independence, 1776

The lofty promises of the Declaration of Independence were written by white people for white people. Life, liberty, and the pursuit of happiness were never intended for African Americans or any other people of color in this nation. But that doesn't mean they haven't tried to attain them anyway. At every step along the path of American history, you can see resisters of racism attempting to make the promises of the Declaration available for everyone. That resistance has had low points and high points. All too often, it seems as if struggles for justice are on their last breath,* and the struggle becomes one to just stay alive. But there are other times when it seems the path is leading somewhere and hope and victory are just around the corner.

Racism's Self-Protecting Pattern

In chapter 1, we identified two brief periods in our nation's history when an exciting forward movement took place in the struggle against racism—the Reconstruction era following the Civil War (1865–77) and the Civil Rights Movement, "the Second Reconstruction era"

---

* This is reminiscent of the dying words of George Floyd ("I can't breathe"), a man strangled to death on May 25, 2020, by Minneapolis police officer Derek Chauvin.

(1954–68). Both these historic moments were brief and were jolted to sudden endings when the forces of racism in our nation decided things had gone too far. While a great many positive steps were taken during these two periods, the roots of racism that lie at the heart of our nation's structures did not sustain lasting damage.

Our goal in this chapter and the next is to explore what we believe to be a common pattern of racism's behavior and the resistance to it during these two Reconstruction periods. The frustrating reality is that racism doesn't go down and stay down. It always picks itself up, shakes itself off, and comes back, reasserting itself in a new suit of clothes.

Before the Pattern Began

Although this pattern of racism and resistance did not begin until the First Reconstruction era in 1865, we need to affirm that resistance to racism has always existed in this nation. Prior to the First Reconstruction era (1865–77), resistance was primarily focused on the need for survival. Enslaved Africans resisted on the ships that carried them like sardines packed in a can, and their resistance continued once here. This included armed struggles waged for freedom. The false narratives that Africans came gently, softly, and quietly to their enslavement and that Indigenous people were savages whose only goal was to stop the brave settlers arriving to make America great are useful lies for those who want to maintain control.

Resistance took many forms. The Underground Railroad was a critical example of resistance, as was the abolitionist movement. We can only imagine how many untold and undocumented stories of courageous resistance fill the years from 1619, when the first Africans arrived on these shores, to 1865, when enslaved Africans became legally free. Prior to the First Reconstruction era, racism had securely rooted itself as the foundation stone on which this nation would be constructed, and every system was designed with the ideology of white supremacy sanctioned in the nation's Constitution.

This white supremacist worldview was embodied, embedded, and cemented in every one of this nation's systems.

The Pattern Begins

During Reconstruction, the focus of resistance turned to racism's roots, and the real struggle for eliminating racism began. We see the emergence of a repeating pattern of interaction between the forces of racism and the forces of anti-racism. This pattern demonstrates how, despite the resistance, the roots of racism remain untouched. As we shall see, when this pattern is in place, resistance challenges racism at root levels, but the forces of racism are able to halt anti-racism's challenge to systemic racism before it is able to bring about in-depth transformational change. Responding to the threat of anti-racism efforts, racism and racist practices allow transactional changes (superficial changes) that create an illusion of change that maintains a balance of racism and resistance while protecting at any cost the extended power of white supremacy.

By studying this pattern of behavior before, during, and immediately following the two Reconstruction periods, the effectiveness of the pattern becomes apparent. This pattern allows enough transactional change to satisfy the pressure of anti-racist resistance while at the same time preventing the deeper transformational change required to undo racism. In addition, racism maintains the ability, when pressured, to apply the brakes hard, to stop or redirect resistance.

So long as this pattern is allowed to continue, decisions about when and how much to change remain in racism's hands. Unless these patterns are broken and means of prevention are developed, a Third Reconstruction era will suffer the same fate. In chapter 5, we will provide concrete steps toward the deconstruction of systemic racism, bringing what we hope and believe will be a part of the coming third period of Reconstruction. But here in chapter 3, we need to study more closely the previous attempts at Reconstruction and the anti-racism response so we can better comprehend the pattern that sees racism's leaves torn and branches broken and yet leaves the deep roots of white supremacy barely touched.

How the Pattern Works

The pattern has four distinct steps:

1. *Reconstruction.* Dramatic progress in countering racism is made in many public race-related issues. This progress reveals itself in many ways: civil rights legislation, increased numbers of people of color elected to public office, people of color advancing in leadership positions in business, industry, the arts, and media. Racist reactionary public figures are less visible. There is a positive shift in the public mood with a sense of celebration and positive expectations about the future.

2. *Ending of Reconstruction.* With roots of racism left intact, conservative and reactionary responses to positive accomplishments and moods begin to surface. Candidates expressing alarm and dissatisfaction with progress are elected to office, and there is a sharp downturn in the public mood. With the resulting loss of momentum in positive accomplishments, reconstruction is brought to a halt.

3. *New forms of racism.* Racism resurfaces, and a sense of loss permeates communities of color. New and increasingly sophisticated forms of systemic racism appear.

4. *New forms of resistance.* As new forms of racism grow, new forms of resistance counter, pushing again toward reconstruction.

Let us next highlight each step of the pattern during the previous Reconstruction eras. Understanding the pattern is key to making the Third Reconstruction one that can last.

THE FIRST RECONSTRUCTION ERA: THE PATTERN BEGINS

Reconstruction without Deconstruction

The Reconstruction era, a brief period from 1865 to 1877, was the first great step forward in the pattern of struggle between racism and anti-racism. For the twelve years following emancipation, the anticipation and hope for real freedom ran high. *Jubilation* is even a mild word given the expectation and hoped-for outcomes in this period of Reconstruction. After centuries of enslavement, imagine, if you dare, what that must have felt like, if only for a moment, to be told that you are truly free.

This was a time of great hope for recently freed Africans. For the first time, African Americans and other people of color were allowed a peek through the window to the freedom that was just on the other side. This period of Reconstruction brought hope in the form of amendments to the Constitution: the Thirteenth Amendment (legal freedom for previously enslaved Africans), the Fourteenth Amendment (citizenship for formerly enslaved Africans and others), and the Fifteenth Amendment (voting rights for African American men). This First Reconstruction era set in motion a long and arduous struggle to acknowledge people of African descent as fully human. Indelible changes were made to create a just nation for all people. The wonderful words "life, liberty, and the pursuit of happiness" represented ideas for which legally freed Africans had fought, prayed, and hoped.

However, this was also a time of great disappointment. The First Reconstruction era lasted just long enough for white supremacists in the North and South to come to the terrifying awareness that the cumulative empowering effects of emancipation on the newly freed enslaved Africans were on the verge of successfully transforming the country into the radical democracy that the Constitution presumably originally intended. A chorus of white voices shouted, "We didn't mean to go that far!" White power stepped on the brakes with a singular goal in mind: to stop Reconstruction. And in 1877, twelve years after it began, the First Reconstruction was ended. As we have observed, when in full control, racism will act out its mission of maintaining white supremacy in overt and virulent ways. But we have also seen that when racism is exposed and needs to hide, it will create another image of itself and pose as a friendly ally.

By 1877, with the Hayes-Tilden compromise, the South was given full authority to reconstruct itself. The presence of federal troops in the South, which had been a liberating and protective force for legally freed Africans, was ended. These troops were replaced by reestablished oppressive and violent grassroots police forces ruling by intimidation and murder, including the Ku Klux Klan (KKK). The abandonment by the federal government of the legally freed Africans allowed the South to "rise again" as it said it would. The First Reconstruction era ended with racism fully intact.

Post-Reconstruction: The Creation of New Forms of Racism (1877–1954)

Racism had been knocked down but not out. In 1896, the Supreme Court's ruling in *Plessy v. Ferguson* became the final nail in Reconstruction's coffin. In short, this ruling created a separate but equal doctrine that led to various forms of segregation. Public facilities such as trains, buses, hotels, theaters, and even schools could be, and often were, sanctioned as separate for Blacks and whites. This ruling gave permission at every jurisdictional level for an American system of apartheid dressed as "Jim Crow" to allow racism to regain and maintain control. America's systems and institutions still benefited white people exclusively, with no real deconstruction of racism having taken place in the systems of this nation. This era of US history introduced changes that were bitter and sweet. Enslaved Africans had come close to freedom, but it was not actualized. Visions of racial justice remain unfulfilled.

With the demise of Reconstruction, it became clear that this nation was not about to construct new foundations for democracy. Rather, it reconstructed old foundations of white supremacy by replacing slavery with other forms of racial domination. New forms of racism gave white people ongoing control of Black people, and few limits were placed on the acts of violence required to maintain this control. The Jim Crow / apartheid system remained the law of the land for seventy-seven years until 1954. During this time, a multitude of new laws were created locally and nationally to strengthen the roots of racism and maintain white supremacy. This new form of racism opened the floodgates for anybody and everybody to abuse Black people. With Jim Crow / apartheid in place, in many places, white people could kill or abuse Black people with little if any consequences. Lynchings of Black people—men, women, and children—were sporting and church events. Mass murder and the destruction of entire Black towns and communities occurred. Some of these assaults include the Tulsa Massacre in Oklahoma in 1921, the Rosewood Massacre in Florida 1923, and what came to be known as the "Red Summers" in 1917 and 1945 when Black soldiers returning from World War I and World War II were lynched. The entire legal system was used as a brutal weapon in the arsenal of those who would uphold white supremacy.

New Forms of Resistance to Racism

But resistance was not giving up. It became increasingly clear to Black people that if real freedom was to happen, they were the ones who would have to make it happen. During these seventy-seven years, new forms of resistance were created not only to survive Jim Crow / apartheid but to get ready for the next big push toward freedom. For the sake of life and liberty, many Black people engaged in a great migration to the North. Many had to steal away under the cloak of darkness, just like their ancestors who had escaped slavery.

Resistance was sometimes organized and sometimes not, yet it moved with courage and grace under many names and in many ways: the Great Migration; the Harlem Renaissance; the National Association of Colored Women's Clubs; the *Chicago Defender* newspaper; the antilynching movement, led by Ida B. Wells-Barnett; the founding of Howard University, specifically its law school; the founding of Tuskegee University; Panhellenic councils; the *Green Book*; the National Association for the Advancement of Colored People (NAACP); the Brotherhood of Sleeping Car Porters; and a plethora of others. As we will discuss further in the next chapter, this was also the time of African Americans breaking away from white Christian denominations and the founding of independent African American churches and denominations. These Black churches and religious organizations became the bedrock of the Black community for those who left the South, as well as for those who stayed or could not leave. Many independent African American businesses and communities were also part of the resistance in preparation for the struggle of the next Reconstruction era.

THE SECOND RECONSTRUCTION ERA (1954-68)

The Pattern Comes Full Circle

The Second Reconstruction era, better known as the Civil Rights Movement, rode the crest of the wave of resistance to apartheid and continued the effort to reshape the identity of this nation. The new push forward was guided by the wisdom of the elders and led by the creative vitality of the youth. The Civil Rights Act of 1964, the Voting Rights Act of 1965, and the Fair Housing Act of 1968 are still today the platforms from which much of the battle for racial justice is fought. The philosophy of nonviolence created the foundation on which this movement stood. The commitment, will, and perseverance of this movement are unmatched in this nation's history. The Civil Rights Movement exposed to the world the contradictions of who this nation said it was versus who it really was. The twisted sense of right and wrong reflected in this nation's treatment of Black people was being challenged morally and legally. This nation was laid bare to the world and forced to acknowledge its false identity. As a nation, we defended and encouraged democracy and freedom for people and nations around the world, but we were not a place that embodied these ideals for all its own people.

We wholeheartedly agree with the Reverend Dr. William Barber in his book *The Third Reconstruction* when he says, "As a mass movement, we can pin the beginning of the Second Reconstruction to two specific events: The Supreme Court's *Brown v. Board of Education* decision in 1954, and the murder of Emmett Till, in 1955."* The second big push that the people had been working and waiting for since 1877 had arrived. Like the period of Reconstruction following the Civil War, the fourteen-year Civil Rights Movement

---

* Barber and Wilson-Hartgrove, *Third Reconstruction*, 118.

brought a time of great hope and turbulence and an unyielding defiance of racism. This Second Reconstruction era was filled with drama, confrontation, and enormous changes on the face of American society.

This time of confronting racism is often referred to as a "nonviolent movement for social change." The word *nonviolence* is often heard in ways that have socialized many of us to become numb and desensitized to the inhumane and horrific violence committed against those who were nonviolent. We must always remember to add to the narrative of the nonviolent movement the violence that nonviolent protesters faced. In the United States of America, violence has been the most accessible and utilized weapon in maintaining the white supremacy construct. Racism and those who defend it are some of the most violent forces in this nation and the world. All forms of racism are violent in a very real sense, whether they inflict physical pain, emotional trauma, or economic hardship.

It seemed like victory could be won. But the pattern of systemic racism was not ready to change. After a brief fourteen years of struggle filled with victories and defeats, the death of the Second Reconstruction was at hand.

The Second Reconstruction Ends and the Pattern Continues

A rifle shot rang out in Memphis on April 4, 1968, killing Dr. Martin Luther King Jr. and signaling the beginning of the end of the Second Reconstruction. For more than a decade, beginning with Dr. King's assassination, the nation seemed to wander back and forth in a state of traumatic shock. The era ended with many leaders of the movement being murdered, imprisoned, or exiled. The FBI Counterintelligence Program (COINTELPRO) and the standoff at Wounded Knee in 1973 led the list of violent concluding events. The extraordinary sacrifices, contributions, and stories of those who fought for freedom must never be forgotten.

Nonetheless, when we look back at the end of the Second Reconstruction / the Civil Rights Movement, we recognize that the changes accomplished were both valuable and vulnerable. Change was everywhere, but once again, Reconstruction ended without reaching the roots of racism. The nation desegregated but failed to integrate. As the end of Reconstruction progressed and the post-Reconstruction period began, there was a great deal of experimentation with the implementation of desegregation laws. Bussing, which was done to increase integration, caused great emotional distress; sometimes it seemed to work, and sometimes it was judged as a total failure. The Supreme Court weighed in with the 1978 Bakke Decision and delivered what to some people seemed like double-talk. The court declared affirmative action constitutional but invalidated the use of racial quotas.

The nation had grown tired of the civil rights marches and the demands for change voiced by racial justice advocates and other groups, including those for women's, LGBTQ, and differently abled rights and antiwar protesters. Those who continued to demonstrate for civil rights and an end to the Vietnam War were put on notice. The killing of white students in 1970 at Kent State University in Ohio and the killing of Black students in 1972 at Southern University in Louisiana sent a loud and clear signal that protesting the institutions and policies of this nation would no longer be tolerated.

POST-RECONSTRUCTION (1968–PRESENT): THE PATTERN CONTINUES

With the end of the Second Reconstruction, the movement for racial justice moved into the post-Reconstruction stage. The struggle for racial justice was showing deep signs of weariness. Today, it would be called post-traumatic stress disorder. Barbara recalls the feelings of those days:

> The movement had been made more fatigued by the loss of so many of our leaders. When we expressed our fatigue, Dr. Jim Dunn, cofounder of the anti-racism organizing group People's Institute for Survival and Beyond, would ask us, "What if Harriett Tubman, Martin Luther King Jr., Malcolm X, and other freedom fighters got tired and gave up—where would we be today?" The response to this question was a renewed energy to continue the struggle. And when the old patterns kicked into gear with new forms of racism, the weary veterans of the movement followed soon thereafter with new forms of resistance.

New Forms of Racism Disguised as Friends and Allies

In this second post-Reconstruction era, new forms of racism sneaked up on us, and we were both enamored and bewildered by them. In contrast to the first post-Reconstruction era, in which racism in the form of Jim Crow / apartheid and the KKK made no effort to disguise its hate-filled violence, this second time around, racism made itself look and sound friendly and caring. As we look more closely today, from the perspective of more than forty years later, it is easy to see why many of us were confused. The friendliness was a thin cover for the old ways of rejection and control.

The first way in which racism re-created itself was in the form of new programs and services in Black communities and other communities of color. In the post-Reconstruction era following the Civil Rights Movement, several systems and institutions that had served white people almost exclusively were mandated to move into the "ghetto" and serve everyone. Every system in the nation began setting up offices in communities of color. What they found when they moved in were communities facing issues of survival. Serving these communities with social programs appeared to be the only solution. These communities received antipoverty programs, housing programs, job training, and child and family services, to name just a few. These programs were developed and funded to provide much-needed services that had been historically denied to these communities of color.

Initially, many of us in the movement did not see through the disguise, did not recognize that even though the resources of these programs were truly needed, they were being framed and directed to take the place of the struggle for racial justice. The stated intentions of these programs and services were clear: they were there to address poverty. But before we knew it, poverty and racism were being falsely defined as one and the same thing. The struggle for racial justice became the struggle to acquire and grow programs and services. This is not to insinuate that all these programs were bad or that they did not provide help. But addressing poverty is not the same as addressing racism. And we came to the realization that as much as many of these programs and services were needed, they also created dependency.

Initially, these new efforts to help struggling communities seemed positive. Every system in this nation that was previously forbidden by Jim Crow / apartheid to serve Black people now went through the motions of serving everyone. But, as it turned out, it was a grand illusion. These systems changed little in terms of rooting out racism. The standards of service were still white standards. African Americans and other people of color were sometimes allowed to sit at the tables where decisions, ownership, and control of the programs operated, but they had no power. Racism still was the guiding light by which every system operated. As in the First Reconstruction, the roots of racism were not deconstructed but were allowed to grow on their own terms and in their own ways. As in the First Reconstruction, the changes in the institutions were transactional and superficial but did not get at the roots of racism. We had not yet reached the initial steps of radical systemic transformation required to become an anti-racist nation.

Many of us who at first bought into the flood of programs and services finally began to question what was really going on. Our people were still lacking so much and, in some instances, doing worse. It took time for community organizers and community leaders to recognize that the movement for racial justice was being redesigned, redirected, and renamed to become a movement of social service providers. Moreover, many of these programs, particularly those that provided social services, were run through white intermediaries. We were being trained as community organizers to address issues in our communities one at a time, but as we addressed one issue, others would present themselves that required even more immediate attention. The community organizing training previously provided for us was an important tool, but we began to realize that something was still missing. Unfortunately, most of the training given to community organizers and leaders was conducted from the perspective of white men. These trainers might have had good intentions, but they did not understand, nor did they recognize, the realities of Black people and other people of color living in this white supremacy construct. These men were trained to herd Black people and other people of color into systems that were not designed to provide services to minorities.

The bottom line? What was missing was the ability of the communities of color to own and exercise systemic power. The programs and services imposed on them were designed, organized, administered, and evaluated from outside the community. The understanding of racism was becoming clearer, and its formal definition (*race prejudice + systemic power*) described clearly what was and was not happening. Systemic racism had not been stopped.

The Second New Form of Racism: Multicultural Diversity and Inclusiveness

In the early 1980s, a study entitled "Workforce 2000" by the Hudson Institute, a conservative think tank led by Herman Kahn, alerted the corporate world that by the year 2000, America's workforce would go through major transformation, including the majority becoming people of color. "Managing Diversity" became the popular mantra, first in the corporate world, but by the end of the twentieth century, virtually every institution in American society had adopted the language of diversity and was placing multicultural diversity and inclusiveness among their top ten priorities.

Once communities began to question the impact of the programs in their communities, a second new form of racism showed up wearing the clothes of multicultural diversity and inclusion. When these showed up, we thought they would provide us with the opportunity of full participation in institutions at levels we had never experienced. Many people of color believed that multicultural diversity and inclusion would lead institutions to recognize that they were there or just outside the door and had much to offer. Again, racism caught them off guard. Multicultural diversity sounded good, especially to the Black people and other people of color who were working to break down the walls of exclusion that kept them outside the systems and institutions in this country. In their excitement about coming inside or participating more equitably inside, they had not considered that power would remain in the hands of white people who controlled the systems and institutions. Multicultural diversity and inclusiveness became a tool to maintain white supremacy by inviting other previously excluded groups, Black people and other people of color, to be present within societal systems and institutions while not changing how the institutions operated or who controlled them.

This pattern continues to allow a limited amount of transactional change to satisfy the pressure of anti-racist resistance while at the same time preventing the deeper transformational change required to undo racism. In addition, racism maintains the ability, when pressures for change go too far, to apply the brakes hard and end any movement toward change. As a result, the concept of multicultural diversity and inclusion creates an illusion of change that maintains a balance of racism and resistance while protecting at any cost the extended power of white supremacy.

Another problem emerged during this time: when white people, Black people, and others who had been excluded were at the same table, they did not always get along. Multicultural diversity became a problem instead of a solution. All sorts of education and training programs emerged to equip people to address the problem of diversity. There were relationship-building programs and presentations on managing diversity, prejudice reduction, cultural competence, and color blindness. Some of these exercises or programs might have moved the conversation of diversity an inch, but none of them moved the conversation to the issue of white supremacy. These training programs were customized to enable relational capacities but not to address systemic racism. At times, goodwill came from these interactions, and yet the lives and lack of full citizenship rights for Black folks and other people of color did not improve. This can accurately be called "racist multicultural diversity," since it describes a form of multicultural diversity that is shaped by racist institutions.

The curriculum and activities for most of these training programs provided methodologies to avoid even saying the word *racism*, let alone addressing it. Through the 1980s and the 1990s, multicultural diversity became the safe language and approach used when addressing the racial disproportionality and disparities oozing from the systems in this country. Once given permission to enter an institution to address disparities, all institutional members were required to learn the language of multiculturalism but did not have to acknowledge the impact of white superiority and white systemic power.

Racist multicultural diversity failed miserably and is still failing miserably to meet its own proposed goals and standards. The bodies of people of color were invited to be present in the institutions, but their minds, spirits, and worldviews were not welcomed. Diversity existed, but the power of the institution to change or not change was left in the hands of the white people who controlled those institutions. Even when Black people and other people of color held positions of power and/or authority in an institution, that power and authority were conditional. People of color who held positions of power were not to tamper with the white supremacist construct of the institution. One visible example of this could be seen when people of color were in the numerical majority, but they were not allowed to change the direction of the institution unless sanctioned by the white system that controlled the institution. Any attempt to change the institution to better fit the realities of their community could lead to defunding, delegitimizing, dismantling, and the withholding of resources. A new term was coined to address such an event: "a minority majority." This is akin to the oxymoron *jumbo shrimp*; you may be a jumbo shrimp, but you're still a shrimp. Many realized that being the majority numerically or sitting in a position of power did not impart power. Power in this nation is not acquired by numerical majority or position; rather, it is determined by those who collectively control systemic power. Multicultural diversity and inclusiveness programs and social services provided a way to distract us from the struggle to end systemic racism.

The New Form of Resistance to Racism: Anti-racist Power Analysis

The pattern of racism and anti-racism continues. Following at the heels of these new forms of racism came new forms of resistance. The introduction of an anti-racist analysis gave a solid foundation to those of us questioning the previous approaches to ending racism. A deeper understanding of systemic racism provided a clearer vision of what we were up against. The approach we would utilize this time to resist racism would require a two-pronged interdependent approach. We realized that we needed to take on the systemic nature of racism by organizing in the community and in institutions.

Step One: A New Anti-racist Power Analysis

The first step was to develop a clear understanding of power and its relationship to race and systems. We needed an anti-racist power analysis, including a working definition of racism. This had never happened before for community organizers. Whether or not readers agree fully with the systemic analysis represented in this book, it is important to recognize that prior to the Civil Rights Movement / Second Reconstruction period in the 1960s, a comprehensive collective understanding and analysis of racism had not existed. This is not to suggest that there weren't people out there who had this knowledge, but it had not been organized and articulated for the broader community.

The early definition of racism was *prejudice + power*. However, Stokley Carmichael and others during the Black Power phase of the Civil Rights Movement brought the issue of power to a higher level. Then, a more fully defined anti-racist power analysis was introduced in 1979 by Dr. Jim Dunn, cofounder of the People's Institute for Survival and Beyond. His definition added the word *race* to the previous definition of *prejudice + power* to read *race prejudice + power = racism*. The inclusion of the word *race* in the definition and an in-depth analysis of systemic power were presented with a visual demonstration that allowed community organizers and leaders to see themselves surrounded and held hostage by systems and institutions. It demonstrated through questioning who designed the programs and services in their communities. Although the anti-racism analysis was not yet fully developed, new information was presented that made sense to Black organizers and resonated with the reality of what they knew their communities were experiencing. The answer to the question of what is really going on was emerging from the fog.

The anti-racist power analysis was not difficult for the Black community to grasp, as the seeds for questioning the relationship of power and systems had been planted by the Black Power movement. The unforgettable and profound voices of leaders like Stokely Carmichael (Kwame Ture) had been calling for Black people to think beyond civil rights in the way they were being socialized to think about it. The voices of Dr. Maulana Karenga and others at the same time propelled us to question the concept of race and its meaning beyond color. Fleshing out the idea of systemic power and its relationship to race was a critical concept that community organizers realized must be understood and infused in the work of the movement for racial justice. Thank God there were those who had made and were making the relationship of systemic power and race clearer for the rest of us.

Step Two: New Models of Resistance

The second step was to develop models that could communicate this anti-racist power analysis to community organizers who sought to respond to institutions controlling communities of color and to challenge racist multicultural diversity within institutions. This required looking through the lens of the new anti-racist power analysis. Those who accepted the new analysis believed that racism was evil and cunning, but if you know what racism is and understand how it works, it is detectable, trackable, and deconstructable.

Having this analysis is critical, but analysis alone is not going to build the anti-racist movement to undo systemic racism. The analysis has to be infused into the training of community organizers and shared with the communities they are organizing. This analysis has laid the groundwork for a better understanding and direction for community organizing for the last forty years. The anti-racist analysis was a direct response to the control institutions had over Black communities, as well as multicultural diversity and inclusion being defined as anti-racist. Resistance does not have the luxury of developing its approaches one at a time because the tentacles of racism do not come at us one at a time. A systemic anti-racist analysis that made sense to those suffering under racism was the necessary key and missing link to opening the door to what would lead us to the next great push for racial justice. The next step was to determine how to introduce and integrate this analysis to those who were organizing.

Step Three: Organizing the Organizers

The clarity of the anti-racist power analysis can be traced to the genius of many people. In 1979, Dr. James (Jim) N. Dunn and Ron Chisholm, cofounders of the People's Institute for Survival and Beyond, met in Atlanta, Georgia, with several giants of the Civil Rights Movement, among them Rev. C. T. Vivian[*] and Ann Braden. The meeting was requested by Dr. Dunn and Ron Chisom to gather insight and direction from those who were leaders and foot soldiers in the Civil Rights Movement. They were seeking firsthand information on what more these leaders and organizers felt could have been done, what they would have done differently, and what they thought should be done to keep the movement alive.

The new anti-racist analysis opened the window of opportunity for organizers to examine the impact of social programs and multicultural diversity more closely. The analysis led to the realization that social programs and multicultural diversity programs were not producing any different outcomes for the communities they were organizing. The need for a new kind of organizing for racial justice

---

[*] See C. T. Vivian, *Black Power and the American Myth*, 50th anniversary ed. (Minneapolis: Fortress, 2021).

was awakened. Organizers were to be trained with the skills needed to bring people together, and the theory called for a humanistic approach of building authentic relationships with the communities they were organizing. The new approach would require that organizers present a clear definition of racism and how its roots would have to be removed if permanent change were to take place. As we look back, we now know that these last forty years were a time of reeducation and innovation in preparation for the next great push for racial justice.

The collective genius of Barbara Major, Dr. Michael Washington, Rev. Daniel Buford, Rev. David Billings, and others led to a deeper clarification, expansion, and understanding of the anti-racist power analysis. The analysis did not dismiss the oppression of capitalism and patriarchy but demonstrated that it is racism that keeps them in place. The institute trainers were not only training but applying this analysis to their organizing work. The application of the analysis in communities is what sharpens and makes clear how racism was keeping all of us organizing against various oppressions but is keeping us disconnected from one another in racism's assigned places. Requests from organizations and institutions for the training grew exponentially. These foundational anti-racism workshops based on a systemic power analysis and community organizing became one of the necessary building blocks for an anti-racist movement for racial justice. Much, if not most, of the anti-racist organizing around this country during the last forty years has been done utilizing the anti-racist analysis initiated by the People's Institute for Survival and Beyond.

The coauthors of this book have spent the last forty-plus years or more studying, learning, and unlearning so much about racism. We now realize that racism has the power to alter its identity, confuse us, and show up as a friend so that we don't always recognize it. The friends that showed up as social programs may have offered temporary relief for communities, but they were not truly our friends. They were more like acquaintances. The definition of racism (*race prejudice + systemic and institutionalized power*) was the only definition that made sense of the experience of Black people and other people of color.

With the realization that racism is systemic, we now understood that our struggle for racial justice must be an anti-racist organized effort against systemic racism. The organizing training—with the anti-racist systemic analysis presented by the People's Institute for Survival and Beyond, Crossroads Ministry, and now others—moved the understanding of racism away from individual acts of violence based on race to systemic acts of violence based on race. This nation owes a great deal to many teachers of community organizing for racial justice, and Dr. James Dunn should be added as a top member of that list. In chapter 5, we will pick up the story of the advancement of the analysis and how it led us to better understand how we can interrupt and stop the roots of racism in their tracks.

The pattern that keeps racism in place will not self-destruct; it must be interrupted and strategically destroyed. The next chapter will show how this pattern works in the church. The final two chapters will explore the task of deconstructing racism and open the path to anti-racist reconstruction.

4

THE PATTERN OF RACISM AND RESISTANCE IN THE CHURCH

. . . certain unalienable Rights . . .

US Declaration of Independence, 1776

In chapter 2, we established that the predominantly white Roman Catholic and Protestant denominations have often come down on the side of supporting racism and white supremacy, or they have at least given tacit and passive permission for it to exist through their silence and by looking the other way. The churches predominantly of color—especially the African American churches, born out of poverty and oppression—opposed and resisted racism and white supremacy.

This chapter will further explore the story of these two groups of churches as they followed the pattern of racism and resistance that we described in chapter 3. Our goal is to demonstrate how this predictable and repetitive pattern has persisted in the Christian church and will continue to do so until we have learned how to go deep enough into the roots of racism in the church to deconstruct racism's self-perpetuating power once and for all.

Before the Pattern Began: The Emergence of a White Church

We begin by taking a closer look at the path followed by the predominantly white churches.

Following the history of white churches in colonial America, on the way to the First Reconstruction era, we pass through 273 years of church history, during which time the churches in the American colonies went through an identity formation process that resulted in their becoming, deep within their roots, self-consciously white churches. Most of the predominantly white denominations were churches imported by colonists from their former homes in Europe, and they continued to model themselves as European churches. They were, in a true sense, colonial churches, deeply believing that God sent European colonizing nations on a divine and sacred mission to claim new territory. Accordingly, they believed God promised divine intervention, protection, and rewards for the colonists' sacrificial devotion to the task.

Beginning in the early 1700s, the self-identity of the colonists shifted from "European" to a new category of "white American," and the churches followed suit. For Christian denominations such as the Congregational Church, the transition to a white American church happened relatively quickly, and within a generation, the culture, language, theological self-description, and sense of home had fully transitioned. For other denominations—such as the Lutherans, who had immigrated from Germany and Scandinavia—the transition stretched across more than two centuries. This slow adaptation process can also be seen in Polish immigrant communities and other eastern European Roman Catholic churches. It is still possible today to find Polish neighborhoods in cities like Chicago where this transition has barely begun.

Whether the process was fast-tracked, taking place in a generation or two, or slow-tracked while multiple generations passed, churches of European heritage increasingly portrayed themselves as white churches and found a sense of unity in their whiteness. They invented a new creation story in which America was the new garden of Eden, or a new exodus story in which America became the new promised land. These became the new roots of the colonial church that preached the promises of God's blessings on the new white nation.

A White Racist Church Supports a White Racist Nation

Tragically, the common identity of whiteness in the mainline churches included the belief that God approved of white supremacy. Around this concept, a distinctive American race-based theology evolved in the colonial church, supported by twisted interpretations of the Bible and portrayals of a God who looks upon the white race as a chosen people. A white supremacist church evolved, reaching across denominational lines and theological differences, to become unified around this belief. The white colonial church developed deep and nearly impenetrable roots of racism that have changed little up until this very day. The churches assured their white constituencies that the Declaration of Independence accurately described them as a special people chosen by the Creator, who endowed them with the inalienable rights to life, liberty, and the pursuit of happiness. The exercise of these rights included divine approval of the genocidal war against Indigenous peoples and of a system of chattel slavery that turned African human beings into property that could be owned, bought, sold, and measured as economic assets.

Churches of Color Resist Racism

During this period, enslaved Africans organized their own churches, but they had no official standing in the eyes of colonial governments, and they often faced suppression. These churches of the poor and oppressed provided a spiritual and cultural refuge where enslaved Africans could maintain strength and the ability to survive under almost unbearable conditions. Most importantly, this "underground" church provided a base for organizing resistance. This sacred story of the informal and unofficial church of color expressed an alternative understanding of the will of God. A different gospel message was preached by this church. The message to its members directly contradicted the message of the official colonial church. The message claimed God's just concern for the poor and outcast and rejected and resisted the teaching of racial supremacy. This message eventually evolved into a divine mandate to represent the will of God in the struggle against racism in the nation as well as in its counterpart, the white colonial church.

This grassroots anti-racist church brought solace and a vision of freedom to uncounted numbers of enslaved Africans, with the greater part of its activity taking place in a silent, even hidden way. *Hidden* is the appropriate term to describe the church among the enslaved Africans, since its existence was often strictly forbidden. Worship services were held in secret. Some churches secretly helped enslaved Africans to run away. The sacred music of the spirituals birthed in these churches still inspires the world today. We can see illustrations of the language of secrecy in these spirituals: "steal away," "I'll fly away," and "coming for to carry me home." These spirituals are an early indication of a theology of liberation that is still evolving in the church today.

By contrast, particularly in the northern colonies, the abolitionist movement was neither secret nor silent. White Christians, especially Mennonites and Quakers, joined a growing population of ex-enslaved Africans to develop their own form of American theology, making antislavery their principal doctrine.

In the mid-1800s, as the struggle to end slavery accelerated, the mutually opposing messages of the white colonial churches and the churches of the poor and racially oppressed also intensified. The predominantly white churches, for the most part, remained loyal to the forces of white supremacy, publicly supporting (or at the very least silently obeying) the accepted norms regarding slavery. Except for the Quaker and Mennonite churches, few white denominations publicly opposed slavery. White Christians who participated in the abolitionist movement often did so as individuals, as they were not able to represent their churches officially.

The White Churches Divide over Emancipation

Then, almost without warning, there developed some serious cracks in the wall of white racist Christian solidarity. Just before the beginning of the Civil War, when legalized slavery was already teetering, the Northern portion of some white denominations came down officially on the side of ending slavery. The result, with long-lasting effects, was a split within some of these predominantly white denominations, creating Northern and Southern versions of several Protestant denominations (i.e., Northern and Southern Baptists, Methodists, Presbyterians, etc.). This new configuration within the white church had the temporary positive effect of helping to foster acceptance of emancipation by the Northern states. And for a short time following the bloody Civil War, there was a strange temporary alliance between Northern white denominations and churches of color. This alliance made important contributions to the period of Reconstruction, helping to build a spirit of renewal and reconstruction while giving—at least for a moment—public acceptance and credence, partnership, and a moment of strength and support to the churches of color.

READER'S REFLECTION

Others have noted a remarkable spiritual similarity between the Church of the Oppressed during the time of American slavery and the resistance of the Confessing Church of Germany in the 1930s and 1940s. Both churches stood in courageous opposition to a majority church that gave its loyalty to white supremacy. Confessing Church theologian and martyr Dietrich Bonhoeffer, visiting New York City's Harlem community and churches in the 1920s, found life-giving theological expression for his growing understanding of what it means to be an obedient servant of God.* Who in your denomination would you identify as an inspirational model-resistor of racism?

Prayer suggestion: Give thanks for those with courage to stand against racism.

---

* Dietrich Bonhoeffer was a Lutheran pastor, theologian, martyr, and leader of the Confessing Church that resisted the Nazi regime. He was executed a few weeks before the end of the war for his participation in a plot to kill Hitler. See Reggie William's study of Bonhoeffer's *Black Jesus* in the Bibliography

THE CHURCH AND THE FIRST RECONSTRUCTION PERIOD

When the end of slavery was finally mandated in 1865, the First Reconstruction era began, and the pattern of struggle was undertaken to alter the roots of racism in the church. A head-on collision between the forces of racism and the forces of anti-racism became inevitable.

At the same time, these denominational divisions contributed to deepening the gulf between the North and South. And then, when Reconstruction ended with unpredicted rapidity, the white churches in the North and South began the long process of coming back together again, rediscovering common purposes in advocating and protecting white supremacy, supporting Jim Crow segregation, and restricting the freedom of freedmen. Thus began the mission of reestablishing relationships that had been broken at the time of emancipation and rebuilding alliances that had created and strengthened the bonds of white supremacy within the white church. This reunification lasted through the period of post-Reconstruction and, in some cases, even during the time of the Civil Rights Movement.

READER'S REFLECTION

Can you trace your denomination's history back to the Civil War split? Are you from a denomination that has, or in former times did have, the word *northern* or *southern* in its name? If so, do you know the history behind the name? It may mean that your denomination chose sides "for" or "against" slavery and emancipation. Do you know someone who knows the story? How does that affect the way your denomination stands today on issues of race and racism?

The Black Church and Reconstruction (1865–77)

Emancipation! It was the moment that the Black church had been waiting for, preparing for, and praying for. It released pent-up energies and creative forces that gave substance to the Reconstruction era. The air and spirit of freedom along with a new brand of leadership sent an electrifying jolt throughout the nation from north to south. The Reconstruction era brought excitement and creativity to the Christian church that had seldom been experienced in its nearly two-thousand-year history. Black congregations that had existed in secret were able to celebrate and publicly unveil their existence. These congregations quickly became the center of life for the newly unbound Black communities. Black churches multiplied in number and celebrated freedom as a gift from God. They served as community centers and mutual aid societies, and they became centers of creativity for Black entrepreneurship, social gospel, and cultural arts, including that of the famed Harlem Renaissance. With unsurpassed energy, the newly freed church leaders contributed to the shaping of Black political leaders. Black people began winning elective political offices in the first years of freedom with overwhelming support from the Black churches.

But as we have already observed, Reconstruction didn't last long enough to affect permanent change. The white church and society felt threatened by the Black church's creative surge, and Reconstruction quickly came to an end. African Americans were targeted with Jim Crow / apartheid, while the Ku Klux Klan became the enforcers of a new form of slavery. The Black churches were forced to adopt a self-defensive position and, in some cases, went back into hiding. Still, they carried with them into the post-Reconstruction life a vision of freedom and a determined spirit of resistance and rebellion that would guide them during the next seventy-seven years as they prepared for the next period of revolutionary change on the distant horizon—the Civil Rights Movement, also known as the Second Reconstruction era.

THE CHURCH IN THE POST-RECONSTRUCTION ERA (1877–1954)

The lengthy post-Reconstruction period featured the punishing invention of new and cruel forms of racism as Jim Crow / apartheid became the law of the land. During Reconstruction, the Black church had reflected the spirit of freedom and was filled with exuberance and optimism. But now, as Reconstruction was forced to a halt, the freedmen were experiencing defeat. A hard lesson had to be learned; white supremacy was not going to surrender quietly, and true freedom was not going to come easily. The fight for freedom had a long way to go.

But as the saying goes, heat tempers steel. Out of the experience of failure came a stronger people in a stronger church. Amid deeper suffering, the Black church prepared to struggle against giants. The withdrawal of the federal troops from the South, the Supreme Court's decision in *Plessy v. Ferguson* to legalize segregation, the re-empowerment of the same Southern leaders and defenders of slavery who had originally led the Confederacy into Civil War, and the rise of the Ku Klux Klan and other enforcers of racism left the Black community with the frightening prospect of being left to fend for themselves.

The Reinvention of Resistance in the Black Church

And fend for themselves is what they did. With little support from the outside and meager resources on the inside, the Black church created a way of life that made survival possible. The Black church became one of the strong anchors on which the Black community depended to re-marshal forces, gather new strength, and stand in opposition to the forces of Jim Crow. The Black church played a strong central role, providing both the leadership and the sanctuary to make survival possible for the next seventy-seven years. They not only kept their eyes on the prize but developed the strength and direction to prepare for the Second Reconstruction. At the center of this organizing for survival and new life was a dynamic theological understanding of the Christian message that refused to let hope die.

READER'S REFLECTION

If your congregation or denomination identifies itself as part of the historic Black church, how do you celebrate or observe holy days in remembrance of those days of struggle? How do elder members recall this period in your church?

The Resurgence of Racism in the White Churches

Meanwhile, in the predominantly white churches, a different kind of return to normalcy was being experienced. As noted earlier, just before emancipation, the Northern branches of some of the most influential white denominations had shifted their position and publicly advocated for the end of slavery, resulting in a break in their relationship with their Southern counterparts. Now, with the end of Reconstruction and the incoming of Jim Crow / apartheid, many of these Northern churches went back repentantly, with tail between their legs, to reach out and repair the breach between themselves and their Southern counterparts. During the rest of the post-Reconstruction period, the reunified white churches in the North and South mostly obeyed and supported the nation's policies and upheld practices of racial segregation and white supremacy.

The Social Gospel Movement Ignores Racism

During the period of 1870–1920, one of the most important movements in the history of the American Protestant churches took place—the Social Gospel movement. In a manner that had never happened before, the beliefs and practices of Christianity were taken beyond the singular focus on individual salvation to address social problems such as poverty, economic inequality, urban squalor, women's suffrage, militarism, child labor, alcoholism, and more. Leaders of the movement included Congregationalist minister Dr. Charles Monroe Sheldon, Baptist preacher and theologian Walter Rauschenbusch, and Jane Adams, creator of the first settlement house in Chicago and the first American woman to win the Nobel Peace Prize.

The Social Gospel movement took place in the middle of the first post-Reconstruction era, when racism in the form of Jim Crow / apartheid had reached its cruelest expression ever. Even though some church leaders attempted to relate the social gospel to race issues, the Social Gospel movement took place mostly inside a white bubble. It was for the most part a segregated movement in which white churches focused on Christian charity and justice to solve the needs of white people. Nevertheless, thirty years later, leaders of the Civil Rights Movement, including Dr. Martin Luther King Jr., were greatly impacted by the teachings of the social gospel and applied them to the struggle against racism.

A White Mini-minority Takes a Stand against Racism

One more positive sign became increasingly visible during the latter part of this post-Reconstruction era. Most of the predominantly white church denominations unquestioningly accepted their positions of white privilege in society, taught white superiority as biblical truth, practiced racial segregation in their congregational worship, and were silent about societal racial injustice.

Nevertheless, each denomination had a small but energetic cadre of white people who publicly opposed racist teachings and practices in church and society. These leaders were not often found living out their convictions within their home churches, but rather they went out from their churches to contribute as leaders in organizations such as the NAACP and the Fellowship of Reconciliation and in the legal community, where they were preparing for the day when segregation would not survive legal challenges. Their contributions are noteworthy, not because their efforts effectively hindered the forces of racism, but because those efforts were a courageous witness when it was not popular to do so. And we will see later in this historical summary that their influence is still being felt today as we prepare for the third period of Reconstruction.

READER'S REFLECTION

Do you consider your congregation to be part of the white church? What can you find out about the role of your denomination in the time of segregation? What did your church teach? What were its practices? How were lies about white supremacy and the inferiority of people of color taught in the church? Who resisted/opposed racism?

THE CHURCH AND THE SECOND RECONSTRUCTION ERA (1954–68)

The Civil Rights Movement, also here identified as the Second Reconstruction era, changed the face of race relations in the United States of America. And although it was slow in happening, it ultimately also changed the face of the church. The fourteen years of the Civil Rights Movement were a dramatic struggle that played out on the streets and in other public places, including the churches. Almost every day brought about another victory or defeat. Perhaps at no time in the history of the United States has the church been more publicly engaged or influential. But it was the Black church that played the most significant role, stepping in when the white church was paralyzed by its loyalty to racism.

The Black church's response during this time was not perfect. Many Black congregations and denominations were overcome by fear and internal dissent just as much as the white churches. Many of them publicly disavowed any association with churches or organizations that identified with the struggle for civil rights. But when racial justice cried out for leadership, it came from Black church leaders, such as Dr. Martin Luther King Jr., Rev. C. T. Vivian, Rev. Jesse Jackson, Rev. Ralph Abernathy, Fannie Lou Hamer, and hundreds more leaders of the Southern Christian Leadership Conference and other Black churches and church organizations. Thousands of courageous young people from the Black church responded faithfully, led marches, and were willingly arrested and imprisoned. They took the lead in the national struggle against racism and white supremacy. A few white church leaders participated in the Civil Rights Movement, but most churches simply missed the opportunity to listen to and learn about an anti-racist gospel and followed a different path. White church leaders who are willing to listen to and follow the leadership of people of color are still desperately needed today.

The Pattern of Racism in the Predominantly White Church

During this Second Reconstruction era, some members of the white churches did try to listen, learn, and follow. When they did, they faced a complex pathway. They were caught between a rock and a hard place. Many white Christians were desperate to disassociate themselves from the reactionary half of our country that stood at segregation's door and cried, "Segregation now! Segregation forever!" At the same time, only a few were ready to join the marches and demonstrations demanding integration.

Over the centuries, the white church had accepted the principles of white superiority and Black inferiority with relatively few qualms and little dissent. They had become quite comfortable using Christian theology to defend white supremacy. Now, increasingly, a new brand of church leaders identified openly with positions of equality and integration, but they rightly perceived their constituency was not ready for such sudden change. Thus, even if increasing numbers of men and women were motivated by their Christian beliefs to participate in the marches and demonstrations, they could not claim to speak for the churches where they held membership. They were limited to describing themselves as individually committed Christians with no mandate from their institutional church or to portray themselves as a new and future church in formation. Examples of such persons abound. Some, like Rev. Will Campbell, a Southern Baptist preacher, were forced to shed their denominational affiliation because of their involvement in fighting racism and other justice-centered issues. Will worked as a field officer for the National Council of Churches during the earlier years of the Civil Rights Movement and later became known for his ministry among members of the Ku Klux Klan.

Others, such as Episcopal seminarian Jonathan Daniels and Unitarian Universalist seminarian James Reeb, became martyrs. Daniels was killed in 1965 while registering voters in Alabama. Reeb's murder took place during the 1965 march from Selma to

Montgomery. Today, at least forty such martyrs are honored for their courage and self-sacrifice.

Still others were like one of the professors where I went to seminary: He was a scholar and historian in the Lutheran Church. He regularly took an active part in marches and demonstrations, including the Selma-to-Montgomery march in 1965, and yet he was able to retain his professorship. He did so by virtually living two lives, keeping a major part of his role in the movement separate and hidden from his seminary colleagues.

A few exceptional white Christian organizations devoted themselves to participation in the Civil Rights Movement. The most notable example was the National Council of Churches (NCC). The NCC was established in 1950 in response to the national and international ecumenical movement that had been evolving during the early part of the twentieth century. The NCC became deeply involved in the Civil Rights Movement, representing the mostly white, mainline Protestant churches that made up its membership. The NCC boldly supported the struggle for civil rights, despite efforts by conservative NCC member denominations to curtail its pro–civil rights stance and activities and despite escalating accusations of supporting communism and threats from some of its member churches to break membership.

The Pattern in the Church Continues: The End of the Second Reconstruction

The list of accomplishments of the Civil Rights Movement is long. Desegregation laws and other civil rights measures were approved to counter racism in voting and transportation. Promises of equality were made by a nation that was very slowly changing its mind and deciding that it no longer wanted to be seen or known as racist, though it was doing so without giving up that part of its racist life that was successfully hidden from the public eye. Sadly, most denominations of the predominantly white churches remained on the sidelines, while others joined halfheartedly, only somewhat supporting and working toward desegregation and equality.

But in the struggle for racial justice, promises made are not necessarily promises kept, not even in the church. The nation ran out of time. The assassination of Dr. Martin Luther King Jr. was a tragedy that signaled the beginning of the end of the Second Reconstruction era. After fourteen years of powerful movement, fierce struggle, and real signs of hope, the Civil Rights Movement ended with a tail-spinning descent into confusion and lost direction. It was almost a decade before a new sense of direction could be detected. The Second Reconstruction period ended in the church in much the same way it ended in other sectors of society—with many changes visible on the surface, but leaving the roots of racism untouched, allowing them to resprout and regrow new forms that would make racism more virulent than ever in the post-Reconstruction era that was to follow.

An Awakened Church: Better Late Than Never

As the end of the Second Reconstruction approached, the predominantly white mainline churches experienced an unexpected twist of history. During the Civil Rights Movement, most white churches sat on the sidelines while the Black church provided dynamic leadership. But as the Civil Rights Movement reached its dramatic conclusion, the white church experienced an unexpected and dramatic awakening and was jolted into action.

Here's what happened. In the days immediately following the tragic assassination of Dr. Martin Luther King Jr., a sense of guilt and regret filled the pulpits and the pews of churches across the country. Those who spoke at the funeral of Dr. King in Atlanta made pledges of reinvigorated involvement, funding, and action. That such words would be spoken at this highly emotion-laden funeral was not surprising. But this time the promises of denominational leaders of mainline white churches had a different sound. They had experienced a "wake-up call." They were ready to respond with an energy that would not be easily dissipated. The final months of the 1960s saw many of their words turned into actions that became a bridge to the future. These actions deeply affected white churches and their race-related programs and ministries. What changed was not the awareness and understanding of racism in the churches; that would come later. What changed was a sharp increase in the will of the churches to do something useful to address the needs of the moment. From the often-silent seats on the sidelines came a persistent question: "What should we do?"

The awakened leaders of these predominantly white denominations looked around them and saw a Civil Rights Movement shutting down in disarray. Many of the movement's key leaders were gone. They were either dead, in jail, in exile, or co-opted into working for newly initiated governmental poverty programs. The marching and demonstrations had come to a halt. The Civil Rights Movement, including especially the Black church, was mourning a lost leader and had little unity around the question of leadership and what path they should follow next. Few answers were to be found to the white church leaders' question, "What should we do?"

It is very important at this point to remember the pattern we are tracing; that is how racism keeps itself alive. According to the pattern, the sudden end of Reconstruction is followed by new forms of racism, and these new forms of racism are followed by new forms of resistance. And then the pattern begins all over again, starting with Reconstruction.

The new forms of racism arrived in the 1970s, but this time with a new twist—they did not look like racism. They did not look in any way vicious and hateful. They were gift wrapped, and they communicated the feeling of loving care. As described in the previous chapter, these gift-wrapped new forms of racism fit into two categories:

1. Programs and services that addressed the needs of poverty-riddled communities of color that covered a spectrum

of issues—health care, education, employment, welfare, housing, and so on.

2. Programs of inclusion and diversity aimed at breaking through historic walls of segregation and exclusion.

The Church and Charity: The First New Form of Racism

This first form of new racism could not have found a better disguise to make it sound like a legitimate part of the church's biblically mandated agenda. Doing good works of charity is one of the most natural by-products of being a Christian. These works include caring for the sick, feeding the hungry, clothing the naked, and setting the captives free (see Luke 4:16–19; Matt 25:34–40).

But charity is not always good, and it can sometimes be oppressive. If the problem is a natural disaster or some form of immediate crisis, then charity's helping hand is most welcome. But if the cause of the crisis is the cruelty of oppression and injustice, then a solution based on charity only adds to the oppression. Charity as an alternative for justice becomes paternalism and a means of furthering oppression. We can name many ways that the church's expanded programs of charity have made the church, wittingly or unwittingly, partners in oppression. Charity often accepts the principle that advocacy—speaking for those who cannot speak—is among the highest good, even if it becomes a means of ensuring that the ones for whom we advocate thereby permanently lose their power to speak for themselves. Charity allows the white supremacist to define neediness as a sign of brokenness and provide further justification for paternalism. At its worst, when Christian theology is based on this twisted concept of charity, it mutes the voice of the God of justice. Charity, as an expression of racism and under the thin cover of kindness, can be far more dishonest and oppressive than racial segregation and separation ever were.

The Downside of Diversity

The second new form of post-Reconstruction racism is disguised under the rubric of multicultural diversity. The goals of multicultural diversity and inclusiveness have been particularly attractive to the churches. Radical inclusiveness, when truly understood and experienced, is at the center of the church's theology. The church welcomes all of God's people, and especially those who are not welcome elsewhere. At least, that's what is supposed to be true about the church. The first and most important foundational principle of Christianity is that every human is a member of the family of God. This message is central to the Bible, from the first book of Genesis to the last book of Revelation.

The reality is that the predominantly white Roman Catholic and Protestant denominations have had a long history of exclusion, and to this day, Sunday morning worship is still the most segregated hour of the week. The long-standing acceptance of their belief that the only human ones are white people has been rooted in the church's self-understanding. The vision of a multiculturally diverse and inclusive church is a profoundly sacred and divine vision, but it is not a present reality in most denominations.

The focus on diversity can be used as a cover-up for deeper forms of racism. Just as charity can be a racist alternative to justice, so diversity can become an alternative to anti-racism. Most denominations have turned to a variety of education and training programs to facilitate the process of becoming multicultural. But these programs do not accomplish their stated goals if there is not an accompanying transformation of the white supremacist roots that made the denomination white in the first place. If multicultural diversity programs are enacted without the larger focus on an anti-racist transformation of the church's life, culture, and theology, then multicultural diversity and anti-racism will become enemies.

A Theology of Pronouns

Here's a simple way of testing whether diversity is a deterrent or an incentive to developing anti-racism in your church. You can tell by the pronouns. When "we" invite "them" into "our" church, there has not been a change in ownership. When it is "our" church, it is not God's church. When it is "our" church, it is "our" standards that people must live up to, not God's.

An extension of the pronoun problem is inherent in the theology of multicultural diversity that is articulated in most of our churches. Not only do "we" invite "them" into "our" church, but we also reinforce the problem when we ask people of color and people of other cultures to leave a large part of their identities outside when they come inside. All too often, our invitation infers that "we hope you will come into our church, but if you do, you will have to accept us and the way we do things; you will have to change in order to become like us, because we weren't thinking about our need to change."* Once again, the issue is power—systemic power. And the problem is that people of color are required to divest themselves of power when they enter our systems.

We see an example of this in the early New Testament church described in Acts, chapters 10–15. Some early Christians thought that new male gentiles coming into the church had to be circumcised to be full members of the Christian church. But the apostle Peter and other church leaders discovered the meaning of the gospel's radical and unconditional inclusiveness. In Christ, people of every place and circumstance are welcomed to "come as they are" into the church. This unconditional inclusiveness asks not how new people need to change to "fit" into the church but how the presence of new people can bring exciting and creative change to the church. If the church's multiracial and multicultural programs insist that new members fit into old molds of church membership, we will

---

* Safwat Marzouk describes this concern in detail in his book *Intercultural Church: A Biblical Vision in an Age of Migration* (Minneapolis: Fortress, 2019).

continue to see the tally of new members of color in our multicultural numbers game fall far short of projected goals and quotas.

READER'S REFLECTION

Most mainline predominantly white denominations have placed multicultural diversity high on the list of activities. Readers may want to do research on their denomination's inclusivity goals to determine whether the diversity campaigns of their denomination are structured to overcome racism or to avoid the hard work of anti-racist transformation.

Resisting These New Forms of Racism

As indicated in the previous chapter, addressing systemic power is an essential key to deconstructing the roots of racism. This is also true for deconstructing racism in the church. Sometimes, when new forms of racism are more sophisticated and complex, the new forms of resistance take a little longer to be created. This has been the case with these two new forms of racism following the Second Reconstruction.

Comprehending and responding to these two forms of racism have brought into being a whole new analysis of systemic racism. This analysis shows how anti-racist, power-based organizing can lead to the deconstruction of racism's roots. The new power-based systemic analysis (summarized in chapter 1) has been developed and shared within many of the mainline predominantly white denominations by the People's Institute for Survival and Beyond and Crossroads Ministry, among others.

Most of these churches at first attempted to juggle the two approaches at the same time, continuing to foster programs of charity and diversity, even while struggling with an analysis of racism that names charity and diversity as expressions of systemic racism. It should not be surprising to learn that attempts to carry out these two contradictory approaches have met with little success. When church leaders faced a choice, they continued with programs of charity and diversity and rejected the approach that identified charity and diversity as forms of systemic racism. Until recently, there was minimal validation of this systemic analysis, with church leaders following their gut reactions and putting a stop to anti-racist training and organizing.

Over the past few years, the directions have once again shifted. It has rather suddenly become "acceptable" to describe America's racism in systemic terms. "Systemic" or "structural" racism has become an increasingly popular way of describing the problem, and "anti-racism" has become acceptable as a way of describing the solution. This appears to be at least partially due to the organizing of Black Lives Matter campaigns, the outcry against police shootings of Black men, and the new Poor People's Campaign led by Rev. William Barber. But it is also part of the long-term effect of anti-racism training by groups such as the People's Institute for Survival and Beyond and Crossroads and the teachers of liberation theology from Black and Latino churches. It is not clear at this moment of writing to what extent this is a sign of acceptance of a systemic understanding of racism. Or alternatively, is it racism's new way of co-opting language for its own purposes of self-perpetuation? The ultimate question is whether we are preparing for the next Reconstruction period, and if so, are we preparing to do it differently this time by going to racism's roots to carry out the task of deconstruction?

In the first four chapters of this book, we have examined how racism took root in our society and in our white churches, and we have identified how systemic racism still exists and is perpetuated.

Reaching the roots of the church's racism and deconstructing them is still a goal to be realized. In the next two chapters, we will turn to describing strategies to help us usher in a Third Reconstruction era that aims at the very roots of systemic racism to bring lasting change.

5

DECONSTRUCTING RACISM

Game Changer

> *Whenever any form of government becomes destructive of these ends, it is the right of the people to alter or to abolish it, and to institute new government, laying its foundation on such principles, and organizing its powers in such form, as to them shall seem most likely to affect their safety and happiness.*

US Declaration of Independence, 1776

We are now ready to directly address the central issue that we announced at the beginning of this book: the deconstruction of systemic racism. We began this discussion with a summary of what we have learned from a long history of efforts to understand and dismantle racism. We have, in fact, learned a great deal, especially as we have examined the two Reconstruction eras. And these learnings have made us much stronger and more capable anti-racism organizers. In chapters 1 and 2, we summarized our learnings about the systemic and structural nature of racism regarding society in general, and then specifically in the church. We especially emphasized the way that systemic racism manifests itself in an institutionalized process that is designed to empower white people and disempower people of color. In chapters 3 and 4, we identified yet newer learnings about racism and its pattern of reinventing itself whenever it senses the possibility of its demise. We believe that every system and every institution in this nation was created originally and structured legally and intentionally to serve white people exclusively.

As a result of organizing during the past forty years, since the end of the Civil Rights Movement, we are heartened to see the increasing numbers of people and organizations who are recognizing the systemic nature of racism and who are supporting efforts to address it. This brings us to the doorway of deconstruction. If we accept that the problem is more systematic than personal, then the solution to the problem must address and bring about change in the way our systems and *institutions* function, reaching into the roots far more deeply than we have until now. We believe that deconstructing the roots of racism is the missing link that has prevented long-term systemic change from taking place.

Our goal in what follows is to provide practical suggestions to describe an organizing path that can lead to the deconstruction of the roots of systemic racism, a path of deconstruction that will lead to anti-racist reconstruction. We understand racism to be a systemic construction that needs to be *deconstructed* in order that a new anti-racist construct can be *reconstructed* in its place. We believe this crucial task of deconstruction was missing in the First Reconstruction era and was also missing in the Second Reconstruction era (the Civil Rights Movement). This absence of deconstruction helps explain the limitations and the impermanence in the changes that took place during both Reconstruction eras. Even more importantly, we believe that carrying out the task of deconstruction is critical to preparing for the coming Third Reconstruction era. Simply put, our primary message has been, *Before we can reconstruct, we need to deconstruct.*

We are defining *deconstruction* as a method of critically examining the level of an institution to expose the roots of racism within its foundation. *Deconstruction* means to dismantle, to take apart or examine to reveal the basis or composition of, usually with the intention of exposing biases, flaws, or inconsistencies. More specifically, by deconstructing race and racism, we mean the process of going to the foundations of systems/institutions where the roots of race and racism are found, and to permanently dismantle them.

As we dive deeper in the process of deconstruction, we believe it will be obvious that not only racism but also the concept of race itself must be deconstructed. If we do not deconstruct race and racism, the space for anti-racist reconstruction inside institutions will not be created. By deconstructing the roots of race and racism, we do mean to permanently disempower them. Like a weed in a garden, the roots must be completely killed, disallowing any possibility of future rebirth. We hope all of this will become clear as we move forward to a deeper explanation and exploration of the process of deconstruction.

An Illustration of Deconstruction

Throughout this book, we have been holding up the US Declaration of Independence as an illustration of a historic document that defines our nation and the principles of life, liberty, and the pursuit of happiness as existing exclusively for the white race. This sacred national document is ineffective for building an anti-racist nation. Our country has tried adding footnotes to the Declaration and similar corrections to other defining national documents, even calling these footnotes by a fancy name—*amendments*. The amendments, some suggest, mean that our nation now exists for everyone. But the original historic document is still intact, proclaiming independence for white people exclusively. In the end, amendments only allude to the inadequacy of an original document and to the need for a new one to take its place.

If we want to be a nation with equity for all, we must rewrite the Declaration of Independence, as well as other sacred national documents. We need to replace them with documents that represent who we are and what we stand for. The rewritten documents must acknowledge our racism and explicitly pronounce that we are becoming anti-racist. And then we need to keep both sets of documents on display to be read and remembered by all so that we do not forget who we once were while we at the same time proclaim who we are now becoming. Read that statement once again, slowly; the deconstruction of racism must leave no question unanswered about who we have been and still are as a racist people and who we are now becoming as an anti-racist people.

Many institutions are not yet ready to receive these conclusions. It will require clear and effective strategy and skilled personnel to get the institution on a journey to become anti-racist. The analysis of anti-racism must be planted and introduced in a way that does not diminish the humanity of the institution's members nor utilize it as a club to beat up on the institution. The work we do for our institutions to become anti-racist is part of building a movement for racial justice. There will always be those who do not want to change. Therefore, a strategically organized effort is required to create a large enough groundswell within our institutions and communities to move us away from engaging in superficial change and to embrace what we will here call "transformational change."

Transformational versus Transactional Change

As we ready ourselves to develop goals and strategies on the pathway to deconstruction, we turn to the subject of transformational versus transactional change to describe the goal of building an action plan for deconstruction. When specialists in systemic and institutional change describe their work, they make a clear distinction between "transactional change" and "transformational change." Transactional changes refer to minor adjustments that incrementally improve but do not significantly alter the institution's structure or functions. On the other hand, transformational change is a deeper change, the kind of change that does significantly alter an institution's structure and function.

If addressing racism was as simple as addressing the individual prejudices of staff persons, the solution would only require that all staff persons be retrained or replaced. Such a change is what we are calling transactional. In the past two Reconstruction eras, efforts to end racism did not go deep enough to get to the roots of racism. As we look back, we see that changes were made. Those changes were transactional changes, which made racism more palatable, but racism was still left in place and in charge. But if we are creating a long-term plan to deconstruct racism that is systemically rooted in the institutional design and that automatically provides institutionalized power and privilege for white people and subordinates people of color, deeper change is required. We are calling this change transformational, a deconstruction process that moves us toward the roots of racism. Transactional change falls short by not measuring the depths of the psychological and historical negative impacts racism has had on people of color. Transformational change includes the recognition of the need for reparations for the damage racism has done.

Levels of Institutional Change

To further illustrate transactional and transformational change, we offer the "Institutional racism levels and change" chart shown below. This chart is designed to help us look at the levels of an institution and better understand how the process of deconstructing racism addresses these levels.

INSTITUTIONAL RACISM
LEVELS AND CHANGE

LEVEL	EXPLANATION	EXAMPLES	TYPE OF CHANGE
PERSONNEL	• People who work or volunteer for an institution • People who are authorized to speak for, act, and implement the institution's programs • People who act as gatekeepers for the constituency and the general public	• Racial inequality in numbers, positions, and salaries • Ineffective training on racism and race relations • Differing treatment of white people and people of color • Lack of community and trust	**TRANSACTIONAL CHANGE**
PROGRAMS, PRODUCTS, & SERVICES	• What an institution provides for its constituency: food, clothing, technical services, entertainment, worship services, etc. • Designed to attract members, customers, or clients	• Different quality programs, products, and services for white people than for people of color • Policies regarding racism and race relations in personnel, finances, facility use, and programs are absent, inadequate, or not enforced	
CONSTITUENCY	• People who belong to or patronize an institution • People who buy products and services • Every decision and action of an institution is taken in the name of and on behalf of the constituency	• Constituency is not representative of community of color • People of color constituency is not adequately or equally served • Outreach to new constituency is discriminatory	

LEVEL	EXPLANATION	EXAMPLES	TYPE OF CHANGE
ORGANIZATIONAL STRUCTURE	• The power of the institution resides in the people in charge, the board of directors, and managers • Where the decisions are made, budgets are decided, people are hired and fired, and programs are approved • Where the boundaries of service are decided	• Geographic or organizational boundaries exclude people of color or ineffectively represent them • People of color do not have commensurate power or authority in institution • Institutional structures are accountable to white people and not accountable to people of color	
MISSION, PURPOSE, IDENTITY	• What an institution stands for and why it exists • Mission, purpose, and identity are defined by constitution, bylaws, mission statement, belief system, worldview, history, and tradition	• The original mission, purpose, and organizational structure exists to serve white people exclusively • The structure, design, identity, values, and worldview reflect a commitment to serve white people better than people of color	TRANSFORMATIONAL CHANGE

© *Crossroads Ministry* Revised 2016 by Joseph Barndt

The chart presents the structure of a typical institution with five levels:

1. *Personnel:* The staff and volunteers who make the institution function.
2. *Programs and services:* What the institution does for its constituency.
3. *Constituency/membership:* The people whom the institution exists to serve.

4. *Organizational structure:* The way the institution is put together and managed.
5. *Mission, purpose, identity:* The "foundations" of the institution; the formally stated reason the institution exists, along with its history and culture.

LEVELS 1 TO 3 (PERSONNEL, PROGRAMS, AND CONSTITUENCY) are the most visible parts of an institution. They are on public display for anyone to see. And they are interconnected. Together, these three present the outer workings of an institution. Personnel produce programs and services for the constituency. Changes on these levels are usually transactional. They are not transformational. They do not change the basic nature of an institution. Transactional change on these three institutional levels may make racism look better or feel softer, or even make it seem like racism is going away. But it will not permanently eliminate systemic institutionalized racism and stop the racial disparities produced by the institution.

LEVELS 4 AND 5 (ORGANIZATIONAL STRUCTURE AND MISSION/PURPOSE) are where race-based identity, culture, and history are found. These levels are less visible to the public, but they reflect the deeper values and areas of institutional control. These are the areas where institutional power is exercised at the deepest core level. It is where personnel are hired, evaluated, promoted, and fired. It is where programs and services are initiated, evaluated, perpetuated, and sanctioned. It's where budgets are drawn up and approved. It is where the mission and purpose are ratified or changed. These two levels are where transformational changes are made and are infused at all other levels.

Transformational change has seldom been approached nor achieved in the struggle to eliminate racism. Transactional change has produced superficial changes, but it is the transformational change we must commit to. Transactional changes—such as making personnel more diverse or requiring programs to have broader, more inclusive application processes—might look good, but they do not touch the area where the roots of racism are buried. Transformational change requires the deconstruction of an institution's race-based identity, race-based history, and race-based culture.

Moving toward Deconstruction

As we have said, deconstructing the roots of racism will not happen without intention and commitment to change. We offer below some strategies to consider as part of a plan for both deconstruction and reconstruction.

Create a Leadership Team

Organizing to become an anti-racist institution is a complex, difficult, and demanding task. We highly recommend that this long-term transformation process be led by a well-trained, officially authorized institutional organizing team. The initial members of the team are those in the institution who have received and been awakened by the anti-racist analysis with power at the center (as summarized in chapter 1) and are willing to accept the assigned responsibility of bringing the analysis into their institution.

Long before this team is officially recognized and authorized, it will serve as an ad hoc committee to work informally toward its eventual formal authorization. For this ad hoc committee to perform its tasks, it must eventually be authorized by the institutional leadership, committed to institutional transformation, and trained with the necessary skills to effectively carry out its organizing task, which is to lead the institution through transformational change. Furthermore, before institutional leadership is ready to authorize the creation of and provide ongoing support for such a committee to build a team, the institutional leaders must themselves undergo training that will unify them in an understanding of the task that lies before them. Our experience teaches us that it can take two years or more for the ad hoc committee to reach the first benchmark of official formation and commissioning of an anti-racism organizing team in the institution. Beyond that, it will require another five or more years to implement the organizing team's strategic plan to deconstruct systemic racism and begin the transformative process of institutionalizing anti-racism. The ad hoc committee and the institution's leadership will work together to determine the organizing team's purpose, authority, size, and representation, and they will outline the team's responsibility to lead the institution toward the goal to become anti-racist and to formally institutionalize, authorize, and commission the work of the institutional organizing team.

Early on in the team's development, there must be awareness that this process is not just for white people and white institutions. The roots of white supremacy are found in many institutions of color as well. The structure and methods by which many institutions of color are organized and operate mimic those of white institutions.

The team members must be critical lovers of their institution who believe in the work and possibility of the institution becoming anti-racist yet recognize that the roots of racism are buried in the institution's foundation. Although the team must be authorized by and accountable to the institution's leadership, many times the most difficult task in the initial organizing efforts of the team is getting the institution's leadership to the anti-racist table to hear and receive the analysis.

The building of an anti-racist organizing team is not easy. The relationship of team members to one another is critical and will determine how strong and effective the team becomes. The nature of the work can cause heightened anxiety and strain on internal team relationships. Because all team members, both white members and members of color, bring to the team table their internalized racial oppression, an external anti-racist facilitator may be needed to assist in resolving issues that are difficult for the team to address on its own.

Build a Strategic Plan

As the institutional organizing team prepares to be moved from ad hoc status to its official appointment, authorization, and commissioning, it will develop a strategic plan to define and carry out its task. As we introduced in chapter 1, the mission and vision of an anti-racist institution commits to the deconstruction of the three cluster roots of racism: race-based identity, race-based history, and race-based culture. The understanding of the vision of deconstructing these roots equips us to carry out our short-term and long-term goal of institutional anti-racist transformation. We now know that race-based identity, history, and culture are embedded in every system, institution, organization, and community in this nation. In addressing the issues of race and racism in every system and institution, we start with this key question: How is the illusion of race rooted in our institution's identity, history, and culture?

The strategic plan will have short-term and long-term transformational goals. The goals of the team's strategic plan will include

- continuing efforts to get a common analysis of systemic racism to as many members as possible, making anti-racism training a requirement for all staff and volunteer leaders;
- providing team members and key leaders with extensive education and training on institutional change;
- building relationships between white people and people of color in the institution;
- developing separate caucuses for white people and people of color to deal with internalized racial oppression; and
- preparing the institution at all levels for the deconstruction of race-based identity, history, and culture.

The institutional organizing team will lead the institution and its leadership to address the following questions: Are we, the leadership of the institution, willing to go through specialized training for institutional and organizational anti-racist transformation? Is the institution willing to invest time and resources in developing anti-racist leadership internally and with communities of color? Is the institution willing to accept wisdom and leadership from communities of color?

The anti-racist organizing principles of the People's Institute for Survival and Beyond, which we introduced at the end of chapter 1 (see pp. 24–26), is the most reliable guide we know for the institutional organizing task. Finally, that which connects the short-term goals to the long-term vision is the achievement of a commitment to anti-racism by a critical mass of the institution's personnel and constituency. Reaching such a critical mass will be a sign that the institution is nearing readiness to publicly acknowledge that it is engaged in the transformative process of deconstructing race and racism and is on a journey to become anti-racist. Deconstruction must be approached with immediacy. At the same time, there is no quick fix, and a realistic time frame must be considered when developing and implementing the strategic plan.

Build the Institution's Ongoing Deconstruction Agenda

In addition to the goals listed above, other possible transformative actions can be taken to further the vision of racism's deconstruction and anti-racism's reconstruction. When developing goals for any given institution's strategic plan, it is important to develop goals that focus on deconstructing the foundational roots of race-based identity, race-based history, and race-based culture. Remaining within these boundaries will assure that the goals are focusing on transformational change and will avoid the superficial trap of transactional change.

Having said that, we want to recommend the organizing team consider three additional goals:

Goal #1: Create a new anti-racist mission statement
Goal #2: Build a new process of anti-racist decision-making
Goal #3: Implement a plan for anti-racist accountability

These additional goals will replace those foundational principles of the institution that have supported the roots of white supremacy. The new anti-racist foundational principles—once collectively determined and accepted—will formalize the commitment to become an anti-racist institution. Let us take a closer look at each of these additional goals.

Goal #1: Create a New Anti-racist Mission Statement

An institution's mission and vision reflect the deepest, most spiritual part of its identity. An institution's commitment to the deconstruction of race and racism and to anti-racist reconstruction must ultimately be reflected in its mission and vision statements. One of the most important, but also one of the most difficult, things to do is to create and affirm a mission statement that explicitly commits the institution to the deconstruction pathway that eventually leads to anti-racist reconstruction. The anti-racist mission statement will articulate a long-term commitment to deconstruct race and racism and to become an anti-racist institution.

A mission statement is not the same as a vision statement. A vision statement depicts the completion of a purpose, while the mission statement describes the pathway of getting there. A mission statement that complements this vision statement will express the commitment of all institutional members to the task of building an institution that rejects the false construct of race and commits to becoming an anti-racist institution. The two statements complement each other and are paired together so that the mission's pathway aims toward reaching a final vision.

The key phrase in articulating this mission and vision is "to become." It will be many years before the process of "becoming" anti-racist can be described as a task that has been completed. Any institution that hurriedly states it has already achieved the status of being anti-racist is making a faulty claim. An anti-racist mission statement must be backed up by a plan for how it intends to get there. Thus, the act of approving these changes in the mission and vision statements is a promise made to the future, a promise that needs to follow and must not precede an institution-wide commitment and strategic plan to go there.

When the institution officially decides and announces its mission to become anti-racist, it must be ready to publicly explain its understanding of anti-racism as well as reveal its strategic plan for how it intends to get there. It will need to clarify its definition of systemic racism and its new commitment to listen to, believe, trust, and follow the leadership of people of color.

Finally, when the word *anti-racist* is used explicitly to describe the new institutional mission, phrases such as "multicultural diversity," "racial equity," or "inclusion" can no longer be used to distract from deeper issues of systemic racism. When an institution decides it wants to become anti-racist, the commitment to deconstruct racism and promote anti-racist reconstruction will be repeated boldly and publicly. The mission statement will also acknowledge the system's/institution's history of racism in order to be thoroughly honest and not perpetuate its historical racist behavior. Anti-racist values will be incorporated in the new mission statement and then will be integrated and infused throughout all levels of the institution. A mission statement can be a cover-up, or it can be a profound guide to anti-racist reconstruction. If you are struggling to create a mission statement, ask for assistance from community-based groups that teach and lead the process of creating mission and vision statements.

Goal #2: Build a New Process of Anti-racist Decision-Making

In an anti-racist institution, not only will different decisions be made, but decisions will be made differently. Our highly sophisticated form of racism has always been able to disguise itself with democratic language, which means that democracy can be used and has been used to perpetuate racism. This was not only true before people of color were allowed to vote; it is still true today, when the vote of people of color holds insufficient power to influence decision-making. In our public balloting for political leadership, in our institutional boardrooms, and wherever else decisions are made, decision-making power is weighted in favor of white people and against people of color.

The decision-making table needs to operate differently if racism is to be deconstructed. Let's be clear and clearly honest: we do not yet know how to do it differently. White people learn very early in life not to listen to or follow the leadership of people of color; it is a learned behavior that is very difficult to undo. Racism is so insidious that it can even be put in charge of anti-racism. Often, white people without an understanding of systemic racism are in charge of our racial justice tables, telling people of color what racism is and defining how it can be eliminated. Here is a very personal revelation about us (Barbara and Joseph) that we have discovered as we share the task of writing this book: although we are close friends and long-standing allies in the struggle against racism, we still need to constantly beware of Joseph assuming the power of decision-making regarding what we will write and how we will write it.

Another danger to look out for is the use of white organizational rules, rooted in white organizational culture, which is not an equitable way to make decisions. Deconstructing racist decision-making may require setting *Robert's Rules of Order* on the sideline. When making decisions, the voices of communities who don't follow Robert's rules are too often silenced. Barbara recalls one of her best learnings from her Black community that was rooted in a question posed by one of its members: "Who is this 'Robert'? We don't know him, so why are we making decisions his way?" *Robert's Rules of Order* is sometimes even required by law to sanction decisions. However, there are other ways of making decisions that can be implemented. The community members on whose behalf we work or who we represent must have a voice with power. When a decision is not sanctioned by a majority of the people of color, the decision should be considered invalid. Organizations are often concerned about the time required to make a decision when the concern should be whether it is a decision that the community of color agrees with.

Anti-racist decision-making must be developed and exercised with more equitable inclusion of the voices of people of color. Anti-racist decision-making processes should be careful not to treat the input of people of color as mere suggestions. People of color must have an equitable seat at the table, where their voices set the agenda and lead the discussion with decision-making power. There needs to be space for innovation, creativity, and experimentation on creating equitable processes for decision-making. A primary standard for ratifying decisions is whether the decision will produce anti-racist outcomes. The system/institution needs to be aware that a democratic process where "the majority rules" does not necessarily guard against continued oppressive decisions.

Goal #3: The Creation and Implementation of Anti-racist Accountability

Predominantly white institutions in our society have not had much practice at being accountable to anyone beyond themselves. Historically, white institutions enter communities of color and implement programs without practicing accountability to these communities. Communities of color have the right and responsibility to reject these unaccountable programs. As we have already noted, all systems and institutions in US society were designed to serve white people. Accountability will require that systems and institutions are uniformly and universally deconstructed and reconstructed with an anti-racist accountability design.

A definition of anti-racist accountability would include a commitment to the vision of African Americans and other oppressed people of color to be self-determined. In the process of deconstruction and reconstruction, white institutions must acknowledge their past racist lack of accountability to communities of color. The ability of an institution to acknowledge its past racist behavior, even if it was unintentional, will determine the degree the community of color will trust the institution's/system's commitment to becoming anti-racist. White-controlled systems and their institutions will no longer have the authority to mandate that people of color be accountable to them without them being mutually accountable to people of color. Anti-racist institutions/systems must be reconstructed with a design that ensures that people of color have the power to hold the institution/system accountable with consequences. Institutions shall commit to not entering communities of color with their programs and services (doing what they please) without obtaining permission from the communities of color. Communities of color will have full authority to veto any decision made on their behalf without their direction, leadership, and sanctioning. Communities of color will no longer be engaged as if they are children to be taken care of by white systems and institutions. They will be respected as full human beings with the capacity to think and act for themselves. Institutional resources will be controlled and distributed equitably by and with communities of color. People of color will claim the power and opportunities to try new methods of accountability without being ridiculed and discounted. White institutions will be held accountable for the education of white people and white society about anti-racist accountability.

Evaluating the Path toward Lasting Change

A new anti-racist mission statement. A new process of anti-racist decision-making. A new way to practice anti-racist accountability. These are three of the most important strategic action goals for anti-racist reconstruction. They provide a glimpse of the possibilities of what anti-racist reconstruction could look like. The pathway to deconstruction leads to the pathway of anti-racist reconstruction. The deconstruction process will make anti-racist reconstruction possible. This work has always been difficult and time-consuming. The path we propose does not necessarily make the task easier, but hopefully it makes some of the distractions and obstacles on our journey to racial justice easier to recognize. We do not claim to have all the answers to all the questions. We are sharing our learnings, our hopes, and the possibilities for this nation.

Any strategic plan undertaken must include an agreed-upon means of evaluating the plan's effectiveness. This evaluation may be new territory, calling for creative invention. For starters, we need to beware of the three ways to measure the presence or absence of racism that have come into being during the past forty years following the end of the Civil Rights Movement. These three ways of evaluation have become accepted as standards of measurement, despite the absence of clear demonstration of their long-term effectiveness. These three evaluation methods are *legality*, *intentionality*, and *opportunity*.

> *Legality*—Civil rights legislation and voting rights acts have
> not demonstrated their ability to permanently prevent or
> correct oppressive race-based behavior.
>
> *Intentionality*—The legal system in this country requires the
> proof of intentionality of racist acts to be the means for
> determining if the harm that occurred was racist. Did
> the alleged perpetrator use the N-word just before
> pulling the trigger? If so, the actions are measurably
> racist. If not, the actions may be criminal, but they are
> not deemed racist.
>
> *Opportunity*—A level playing field is considered sufficient
> to provide equal opportunity and access for everyone,
> without defining what makes a playing field level.

These three methods of measuring racism are important, but we argue that none of them individually nor all of them collectively provide adequate tools for measuring the presence or absence of racism. In the first place, we are asked to utilize race-based measuring tools to measure efforts to eliminate race and racism, and in the second place, these are tools to measure transactional change and not transformational change. We believe that, ultimately, the only true way to measure the continued presence of race and racism in our systems and institutions is by measuring the results of transformational change.

Only by achieving equity in results can we be readied to eliminate race from our vocabulary. So long as it is possible to predict racial group outcomes (white on top, Black and Indigenous people on the bottom, and all other races predictably located in between) within any system (educational, economic, health care, criminal justice, political representation, etc.), racism is still operating in its systemic roots.

Summary and Conclusion

The present American "system" can never produce freedom for the black man. A chicken cannot lay a duck egg because the chicken's "system" is not designed or equipped to produce a duck egg. The system of the chicken was produced by a chicken egg and can therefore reproduce only that which produced it.

Malcolm X, excerpt from his letter to the
Egyptian Gazette, August 25, 1964

The struggle for racial justice has been and will continue to be long and grueling. Nevertheless, we must keep in mind that we are entering onto a new pathway on a journey from which we cannot turn back. Deconstructing race and racism is a new and exciting place to be. We are being guided by a deeper definition of racism that brings new awareness of racism's systemic nature: *Racism = race prejudice + systemic and institutionalized power.*

The very notion of a world without race is too foreign for many of us to comprehend, but when we understand what race is and why it was created, it gives us the impetus to move from the unimaginable to the imaginable. The ultimate mission and vision of the deconstruction of racism carries with it the complete dissolution of the myth of race. Until this takes place, the illusion of race infused in the systems of society will incessantly and intentionally regenerate negative measurable outcomes for people of color. The concept of race is specious and illusionary, but the racism it produces is neither specious nor an illusion. Organizing to deconstruct race and racism within systems must be initiated before new attempts for anti-racist reconstruction can take place.

The decision either to continue on the racist path we are now walking as a nation or to be willing to take a more just and anti-racist path will determine whether we move forward as a nation or implode. The one thing we can say with certainty is that there will be no going backward. We believe we are approaching a Third Reconstruction era. Our learnings from history—along with love, courage, commitment, clarity, and anti-racist strategies—will determine how much farther we will get on the path to build a race- and racism-free, just society. For those of us who do this work as a call to our spiritual responsibility, the next and final chapter of this book offers an anti-racist theological perspective for the church of our day.

6

DECONSTRUCTING THE ROOTS
OF RACISM IN THE CHURCH

*Racism is "the ultimate blasphemy," because it could make
a child of God doubt that she or he was a child of God.
People of faith cannot be neutral on this issue. To stand on
the sidelines is to be disobedient to the God who said we
are created, all of us, in this God's image.*

Archbishop Desmond Tutu, Anglican
Church of South Africa

From the beginning of this book, we have been exploring how every system and institution in our nation needs to be on a common pathway toward becoming anti-racist. It is an elusive goal that was sought in the First and Second Reconstruction eras but both times failed to be achieved in a lasting way. We are convinced that in both cases, the reason for our limited achievements is that we did not set our sights high enough or dig deep enough. We believe that in the struggle against this diabolical power, it is not enough simply to resist racism; our goal must be to permanently eliminate the construct of race.

In this final chapter, we will use the definition and general principles of deconstructing the roots of racism that we established in the last chapter and apply them to the specific systemic setting of the church. We will explore what deconstructing the roots of racism would look like in a reader's home denomination or congregation and describe the contribution that deconstruction would make on the long-term struggle to shape an anti-racist church.

"Taking It Inside": A Path toward Lasting Change

Normally, the direction of the church's mission is to move from inside the church to the outside world. God's people are "sent into the world" to bring the good news of the gospel. We are suggesting a strategy for the deconstruction of racism that moves in the opposite direction. We need to first "take it inside" before we can "take it outside." The church needs to be changing itself before it can help change the world. Later, our long-term goals will call for going back outside to address the larger society with a powerful voice and unified actions toward ending racism and furthering racial justice and equity. But this cannot take place until congregations and other institutional expressions of the church are unified in their own internal path toward anti-racist transformation. Taking it inside means developing unambiguous anti-racist identities and uncompromisingly clear anti-racist voices and actions that are consistent with our religious beliefs and traditions.

As we have seen, when we shine the spotlight of racial identity on the Christian church in the United States, it divides the church into two separate groups, one consisting of denominations and congregations that are predominantly white and the other consisting of congregations and denominations that are predominantly of color. The predominantly white churches have a history of supporting and obeying the rules of racism, and the churches that are made up of predominantly people of color have a history of challenging and condemning the sin of racism. The historic identity of the white churches is grounded in the myth of race and in the assumption that white people can claim the characteristics of humanness that people of color cannot claim. Historically, from the time when the European colonization of North America began in 1492 until the end of the Civil Rights Movement in 1968, the white churches allowed themselves to be used as powerful supports for a racialized way of life. During this same period, churches of color heroically and courageously participated in the struggle to confront and dismantle racism.

Defining the Deconstruction of Race and Racism in the Church

To take the next steps in this journey of the deconstruction of race and racism in the church, we need to make sure we are consistent in applying to the church the same definition of deconstructing racism that we used more generally in the last chapter.

> By deconstructing race and racism in the church, we mean the process of going to the foundations of the institutionalized church, identifying where the roots of race and racism are found, and permanently dismantling them.

Just to clarify, below are descriptions of what this process of deconstruction does *not* mean:

+ Deconstruction does *not* mean addressing the church's racial problems piecemeal, fixing one broken part of the system at a time, or amending one past mistake at a time. We cannot return to any place or time in the history of the church and hit the erase button and move forward in innocence, no longer responsible for actions of the past.
+ Deconstruction is *not* the same as reformation. Race and racism cannot be reformed or improved upon. They must be eliminated.
+ Deconstruction must *not* be seen as a new missionary enterprise in which white Christians from the white church help Christians of color convert to and accept the white church's form of Christianity.
+ Deconstruction is *not* a new program of advocacy or charity or multicultural diversity. We have already established in chapter 3 that programs of advocacy and other expressions of charity, as well as programs of multiracial diversity, are themselves new forms of racism that emerged after the Civil Rights Movement.

Deconstruction demands that we go much deeper to eliminate the roots of race and racism. We will find these roots buried in the systemic foundations of our churches, and we will discover that they have never stopped working in the background to define the supremacy of white Christianity, generation after generation. On the other hand, when the identity, history, and culture of the church are freed from the controlling power of race and racism, the potential for an anti-racist church is enormous. Let's take a closer look at how these concepts are affected by the removal of race.

Deracializing the Church's Identity Documents

What are the documents of the church that have been twisted and have redefined the church as immutably white, perpetuating white supremacy in the identity and actions of white Christians? If we want to be a truly anti-racist church, which of our sacred writings need to be rewritten? How has the Bible been racialized, and how do we deracialize the Bible? How have our doctrine and dogma been racialized, and how do we deracialize our doctrine and dogma? Which teachings, principles, and practices of the church that perpetuate a white racial hierarchy and white supremacy are so deeply embedded in the church's life that we receive them and pass them on without conscious awareness of doing so? How are our racialized identity, history, and culture so deeply bound to self-perpetuation that replacing white leadership with leadership of color only means that white supremacist behavior will be endorsed, carried out, and enforced by people of color? Why is it that we are ready for changes in our words only if there is tacit agreement that the words will not be translated into deeds? What do we need to change in the implementation of our decisions so that a decision to deracialize the roots of our churches will result in the deracializing of both our words and actions? If our sacred documents and doctrines call us to state publicly that we will no longer be a church that defines itself by race, what would we need to do to be able to follow that call?

Deconstructing a Racialized Bible

The first step in racializing our white churches was to racialize the Bible. To sell the idea of race and racism (especially slavery) to society, our Christian forebearers described it as an idea authorized by God. For a racial hierarchy to be accepted, with white people on top and everyone else on the bottom, such a hierarchy had to be in the Bible; it had to be demonstrated that white supremacy was predestined and preapproved by the word of God.

All this had to be invented because such a race hierarchy was never in the Bible in the first place. It wasn't there then, and it still is not there today. We need to be absolutely clear about this: the idea of race, as we understand it today as a function of identity, is nowhere to be found in the Bible. There are many different categories of humanity in the Bible, but there is no racial category. You can search the Bible's images of heaven, hell, and the earth in between, and you won't find the idea of race. There are divisions and classifications by nation, tribe, culture, religion, and language—but there is no mention or category of race.

So if support for race and racism needed to be based in biblical authority, but neither was found in the Bible, then the only thing to do was invent a race-based Bible. And make no mistake, it *was* invented. Slave owners, politicians, and church leaders worked hand in hand to interpret the Bible as race-based, identifying white people as the true people of God and all other people as something less than the people of God. These interpretations were incorporated into the official teachings of most Christian denominations of the day.

For example, in the Old Testament, we had—and still have—the deliberate misinterpretation of stories such as that of the Tower of Babel and of Ham, son of Noah, where it was claimed that these biblical stories portray Black people and other people of color as inferior human beings. And in the New Testament, we had—and still have—references to slavery interpreted as God's endorsement of the practice.

These teachings were passed on from generation to generation. Today, far too many people still associate the idea of race with the Bible, along with the conclusion that racism is the will of God. It is a lie passed on from father to son and mother to daughter that race is in the Bible, that it is God's invention. The existence today of red, brown, yellow, Black, and white churches is rooted in the historical idea of God's approval of racial separation. The web of lies and intrigue that racialized the Bible also created racialized churches that still entangle and confine us. Until the predominantly white church in the United States deconstructs race-based Christian identity, the concept of race and racialized identity will continue to haunt and define the church.

And so, the Bible was racialized, and the first step in deconstructing the roots of racism in the church needs to be the deracializing of the Bible. Understanding how the Bible has been wrongly racialized and used as a tool of racism is one of the most important steps in understanding and eliminating racism in the church. The false belief that race is in the Bible will not be undone until the church publicly, transparently, and repeatedly proclaims it to be a lie that originated in the church and now must be undone by the church. The truth is that there is only one race—the human race. As long as the idea of race is given divine consent, it will continue. It is not enough to say that all races are equal; it must be taught that race is an illusion, a social construct, that it was invented by humans and exists nowhere in the Bible, and it should be nowhere in the church. Until it is taught in every confirmation class, preached regularly in sermons, and repeatedly publicized, confessed, and reconfessed, the lie will be passed on.

Theological Reorientation: Claiming an Anti-racist Gospel

Deracializing the Bible is only the first step in deconstructing the roots of racism in the church. Our separation into red, brown, yellow, Black, and white churches, rooted in Jim Crow segregation, has created a disfigured and dysfunctional family of God. Our long-range vision for the future must include the development of not only an anti-racist church but a church no longer defined by the specious idea of race. A unique feature of a church-based deracialization strategy would be for its anti-racist action plan to contain an extensive amount of theological reflection and spiritual direction. It would be a serious mistake to miss the point that our theology has also been taken prisoner by racism and must be deconstructed and given a leading role in the church's anti-racism action plan. By way of example, here are three central theological concepts that need to be studied, discussed, and adapted as strategic tools for deracializing the church.

+ *Reclaiming an Anti-racist Gospel*

If one point needs to stand out above all others in this chapter on deconstructing racism in the church, it is this: *an anti-racist gospel does not need to be invented. It already exists, hidden among the roots of the Bible and Christian faith.* It is a powerful weapon for anti-racist people. The racialization of the Christian faith is only one of many ways in which the gospel has been and continues to be twisted to favor the rich and powerful and to disparage the poor, disenfranchised, and powerless of the earth. Total and complete acceptance of all people, especially those who are rejected and oppressed by the world, is a root foundation of a Christian understanding of the grace of God.

+ *Liberation Theology*[*]

The great surprise of liberation theology is not God's identification with the poor and powerless. That is already a foregone conclusion for anyone who has been listening to the biblical theme of liberation. The great

---

[*] James Cone (*A Black Theology of Liberation*) and Gustavo Gutiérrez (*A Theology of Liberation: History, Politics, and Salvation*) are examples in a long list of theologians who represented the response of the churches of color to the triumphalist theology of the white church.

surprise is that there is enough grace and liberation for everyone, including the oppressor. Organizers of the process of deconstructing race and racism will need to maintain the point of view that emphasizes the "liberation of the oppressor," not as a means of excusing the long history of white racism that has been present in the church, but rather as a means of consistently presenting an inclusive gospel in which everyone qualifies for the gift of God's forgiving and accepting grace.

+ *The Promise to Resist Evil*

In most denominations of the Christian church, entry into the beloved community is formalized with the rite of baptism. In many of these denominations, the ritual of baptism includes a question that is addressed to the new family member: "Do you promise to resist evil and all its empty promises?" This question and its response ("Yes, with the help of God") mark the entrance into the beloved community as a moment of commitment of one's life to a long list of struggles for justice. This should include the struggle to eliminate race and racism from all places in life, including especially the beloved community itself.

An Anti-racist Church: The Path to the Third Reconstruction Era

As we pointed out in the previous chapter, the very notion of banishing race from our vocabulary and taking on the task of anti-racist reconstruction is difficult for many of us to comprehend. But when we have traveled a way down that road, and the process of deconstruction is underway, anti-racist reconstruction can be initiated with a sense of new possibilities. Reconstruction does not have to wait for the completion of deconstruction. These two processes can happen almost simultaneously, with deconstruction leading the way just a step or two ahead of reconstruction. As the process of deconstruction begins to deracialize identity, history, and culture within the church, the work of building an anti-racist, reconstructed church can begin. By the end of this chapter, we will begin to see what these three concepts—a deracialized Christian identity, a deracialized Christian history, and a deracialized Christian culture—might look like.

Deracializing *Christian Identity*

For Christians, the concept of identity is based on two key questions: *who* we are and *whose* we are. Christian theology teaches that we are children of God, the Creator and Redeemer of all, who claims us in baptism. This identity is not based on race or the color of our skin. Archbishop Desmond Tutu's quote at the beginning of this chapter is a stern reminder that anyone who insists on maintaining racialized identity is giving in to a serious expression of blasphemy against God. Our individual racialization is a dehumanizing process that kidnaps all of us at birth, assigns us to a racial group, and instills a conscious racial identity inside of us. We described this process in chapter 1 under the name of "internalized racial oppression," where white people are socialized into a superior way of life and people of color are socialized into an inferior way of life. We are all socialized to be comfortable with "our own people" and to be uncomfortable with others.

In anti-racist Christian theology, baptism "rescues" us from racism's kidnapping and gives us a seat at the table of the beloved community, where we are equipped to resist the evil one and commit ourselves to the struggle for a just and anti-racist life. At the center of the beloved community stands Jesus, whose identity extends to and incorporates every aspect of what it means to be human and illuminates the fullest humanity in each of us. In Christ, there are no second-class human beings, and there is no race-based identity.

Deracializing *Christian History*

From a wholistic Christian perspective, the recording of human events in time and space merges with God's beckoning toward eternity, thereby making secular history a sacred subject. However, recording and interpreting history in our nation is an enterprise that has been maintained mostly by white historians whose racializing of history causes a distortion of time and its relation to eternity. This racialized categorization of history from a white triumphal perspective is accepted as truth, while the history of the church's global expansion and growth is described as a missionary journey to bring "good news" to lesser human beings.

Deracializing *Christian Culture*

Christians are drawn into relationship with God and with one another in the "beloved community," which is based on a culture of love and justice. All are invited to the beloved community, without exception. The "unloved community" of the rejected and oppressed is at the top of the invitation list. A racialized culture distorts the beloved community, making it into a private club. Christian culture is no longer the true beloved community when it accepts the myth of race as real, natural, and sacred. In the past, and even still today, when people of color join a white church, bringing along with them aspects of their own culture, the white church gives the resultant mix names such as *diversity* and *inclusiveness* and assumes the role of supervising and controlling the mixing process. This is not a true vision of the beloved community.

We need to be prepared for a lengthy and oftentimes complex organizing process to carry out the work of deconstructing race-based identity, history, and culture in the church. Reaching the goal of becoming an anti-racist church and doing the work of anti-racist reconstruction is not easy. This goal can only be accomplished by first engaging in the process of organizing to deconstruct the roots of race and racism. It has taken centuries to create race-based identity, race-based history, and race-based culture in the church, and we need time to bring them to an end. Keep in mind this bit of good news though: while the deconstruction process needs to be underway, it does not need to be completed before the church can move forward to shape anti-racist reconstruction.

Building Leadership and Creating a Plan

The pathway to be followed in a congregation, judicatory, or other institution of the church will in many ways be quite similar to, but in other ways be very different from, that of a secular institution as described in the previous chapter. In the following discussion of the creation of the leadership team in the church and its role in developing the strategic plan, we will seek to avoid repetition of material already covered in the previous chapter. We will add to and emphasize the ways in which the process is uniquely applied for use within the church.

The initiation of deconstruction and anti-racist reconstruction in the church needs to take place on various institutional levels—in individual congregations; in clusters of congregations; on judicatory levels such as in a diocese, synod, or district; and in specialized institutions such as colleges or seminaries. Our assumption is that race and racism have become institutionalized on every level. On the following pages, we will use the phrase "congregation or judicatory level" to address anti-racist organizing work that is applicable to any one of these church institutional levels.

Creating the Anti-racism Leadership Team

As with other institutions, we recommend that the deconstructing work in the congregation or other judicatory level begin with the creation of an anti-racism leadership team. This team will start off as an ad hoc organizing group without formal authorization of its work. Its initiating members will include people with a variety of skills and with long-standing commitment to and experience in resisting racism. The team will require a lengthy period, perhaps as long as two years, before it can build the necessary relationships within the church and community to combat racism and receive official authorization to carry out its institutional role. The leadership team will, during this initial period, focus on its understanding of systemic racism, sharpen its skills in understanding institutional change, and build relationships with leadership in the congregation/ judicatory. All of this will be built on a biblical/theological base and a spiritual foundation as they immerse themselves in the rediscovery of an anti-racist gospel.

When the team discerns that it is ready and when it has created a readiness within the congregation or judicatory level it serves, it will request authorization from the highest level of decision-makers (i.e., church council, board of elders) in the congregation or judicatory and be publicly commissioned to do its work. In building the initial ad hoc team, organizers need to consider which people in the congregation or judicatory have the potential commitment, skills, interest, and temperament to work, plan, and strategize together to initiate a successful campaign to shape an anti-racist strategic plan.

READER'S REFLECTION

If you are reading this book and thinking about anti-racism organizing in your congregation or judicatory, perhaps you would be willing to add your name to the top of the list.

As this new team develops its direction, members of the team will be unified around a common anti-racist mission and a common analysis of racism, and they need to represent a diversity of personalities, ethnicities, skills, and experiences.

The Strategic Plan

When the leadership team is officially authorized, they will be responsible for developing and implementing a long-term strategic plan for deconstructing race and racism and for anti-racist reconstruction. The team will be accountable to the authorizing group that appointed it, and it will also place a priority on helping the authorizing group understand the analysis and support the development of the proposed strategic plan. The leadership team will also receive organizer training and place a high priority on honing their organizing skills.

In developing the strategic plan, the goals and strategies discussed in the previous chapter apply equally to congregations and judicatories of the church. The goals of the strategic plan for congregations and judicatories of the church will include

+ building a shared common analysis of systemic racism throughout the congregation or judicatory—there can be no unified path toward institutional change unless there is a unifying common analysis of systemic racism;
+ providing extensive education and training for congregations and judicatories on the pathway to anti-racist institutional transformation for team members and key leaders of the church;
+ building relationships of trust and mutual accountability between white people and people of color in the congregation/judicatory; and
+ facilitating separate caucuses for white people and people of color to deal with internalized racial oppression.

Moreover, a strategic plan for the church should focus on the three additional long-term goals that we introduced in the previous chapter:

1. Create new anti-racist mission and vision statements.
2. Build a new process of anti-racist decision-making.
3. Implement a plan for anti-racist accountability.

As we turn to look more deeply at the strategic plan for congregations and judicatories of the church, let's begin by focusing on these three long-term goals. Before continuing, however, we strongly recommend that readers review the introductory discussion of these three long-term goals on pages 112 through 117 in chapter 5.

Create New Anti-racist Mission and Vision Statements

The first goal is to create new anti-racist mission and vision statements that reject the false construct of race, repent, and seek forgiveness for past and present sins of racism and commit to becoming an anti-racist congregation or judicatory in which all participants experience equitable giving, receiving, and sharing of peace, power, love, and justice. Contained in these mission and vision statements will be the commitment to strip the congregation or judicatory of anything that could be associated with race-based identity, race-based history, or race-based culture.

This is a transformational goal that will eventually lead to tangible, practical results. For example, when church members learn that "seeing" race anywhere within the church inevitably implies that some races are superior and other races are inferior, every member of the church will face a decision of whether that is what they believe. When church members learn that the Christian faith in general and their congregation or judicatory in particular is moving toward rejecting the idea of race altogether and that Christians are by definition required to be anti-racist, that also will call for deeply personal, deeply spiritual decision-making on the part of every member.

This raises an important question in this discussion of a strategy to deconstruct the roots of race and racism in the church: Can one be a member of the beloved community and not be an anti-racist? As we explore the implications of developing a strategy for the deconstruction of race and racism in the church, at what point is it finally established, once and for all, that there is no room for race and racism still having a legitimate place in the church?

In several denominations (including especially the historic Reformation churches such as the Lutheran and Reformed churches), there is a theological concept known as *status confessionis* (Latin for "being in a state of confessing"). This concept refers to the fact that there can be times when an issue of injustice is so clearly evil and devastating in its results, so obviously contrary to the will of God, and so demanding of unified support for its opposition that the church can declare it a requirement for its members to take a stand. It means that a particular doctrine is essential to who we are as a church. If something is *status confessionis*, it is a "make-or-break" issue. It means that if we are to be faithful in confessing the gospel, we must reject race and racism. When a doctrine or belief is raised to the level of *status confessionis*, the church has the authority and responsibility to pronounce that the issue requires all church members to take a stance of opposition. The most recent time in which this doctrine of *status confessionis* was invoked was among the churches in South Africa during the last days of the apartheid system. This raises an important question: When will it be time to declare opposition to race and racism as a matter of *status confessionis* in the Christian church in the United States of America?

The new anti-racist mission and vision statements must reflect the work of the entire congregation, the whole church. Everyone should be invited to participate in providing feedback so that decisions will be made that represent the whole congregation. The whole membership must face the choice between the unity of anti-racist mission or the continued rewarding of white power and privilege. It is a choice between membership in the beloved community in which everyone is equally a part or membership in a diabolically divided community in which the powerful few exchange their freedom for a trumped-up racial identity. The vision or mission statement is a key to leading the congregation or judicatory toward recognizing its need for anti-racist transformation.

Part of the process of creating a vision and mission statement is analyzing all of the structural levels in the church or organization (see the chart on pp. 106–107 in chapter 5). The articulation of an anti-racist mission and vision originates at the deepest levels of the institution. But it doesn't stop there. It must permeate and penetrate every level, including the levels of personnel, program, and constituency. If institutionalized change is to be transformational, it must originate in the deeper levels and flow to all levels. Efforts to originate change from the levels of personnel, program, and constituency will inevitably be transactional because the roots of change will be shallow and weak. Therefore, transformational change must originate on the institution's deepest level to build the strength required to bring transformational change to every level.

READER'S REFLECTION

Can you identify the five levels of your congregation or judicatory? Or are there a different number of levels? Create a chart that shows the structural levels in your organization.

Build a New Process of Anti-racist Decision-Making

When the church sets a goal to overcome and correct power imbalances, it is on this level that these efforts will be either supported or resisted. Different denominational expressions reveal many different methods of decision-making, some of which place the power of decision-making in the hands of a few persons and some of which traditionally seek to expand the power of decision-making across a more widely representative democratic structure. In both cases, the reality of racism mitigates against the sharing of power. The leadership team needs to be leading the congregation toward an openness to explore new methods of decision-making that are based on white people in congregations and judicatories learning to listen to, believe, trust, and follow the leadership of people of color.

Implement a Plan for Anti-racist Accountability

As can be seen on the levels chart (pp. 105–7), the organizational structure level is the second level where transformational change can be initiated. This is where the power of decision-making is assigned and carried out. It is where priests or pastors and elected and appointed congregational lay representatives follow a constitutionally defined process of collective decision-making. A plan for anti-racist accountability begins with exploring how decisions are made and by whom.

It is also on this level of organizational structure where power is misused in ways that perpetuate systemic racism. Often, the design for decision-making in a congregation or judicatory was originally created and implemented in segregated settings in which white people were socialized not to listen to, believe, trust, or follow the leadership of people of color. Or in many cases, no people of color were present. Few, if any, opportunities or life experiences existed that allowed for racist behaviors to be challenged or changed.

As desegregation began to take place following the Civil Rights Movement, people of color began to be present in previously all-white churches, but white people had no experience or prior instructions on how to exercise power in interracial settings. Still today, the continued reality of racism mitigates against white people sharing power with people of color. White people consciously and unconsciously continue to follow their socialized behavior of not listening to, believing, trusting, or following the leadership of people of color.

The strategic plan of the leadership team needs to focus on this issue. As new relationships between white people and people of color are built, new processes for decision-making need to be explored. These new processes need to teach new behaviors in relationships between white people and people of color. And while these new anti-racist behaviors are being learned, transitional processes need to be enacted that compensate for the imbalance of power. This may require specific training aimed at raising awareness and developing practices of deep listening and power sharing.

The Outcomes We Seek:
Measuring the End of Racism

As we approach the final pages of this book, we need to add a few words about evaluating deconstruction in the church. How do we know if deconstruction is working? We have argued that our inability over past centuries to bring about effective change is directly traceable to the absence of deconstruction. The roots of racism have remained alive and able to thrive. On the other hand, we have claimed that deconstructing the roots of racism makes it possible to deracialize our systems and institutions, to create and shape anti-racist reconstruction, and ultimately, to end racism.

We need to pose the same question we raised in chapter 5 regarding our efforts to deconstruct racism and build anti-racist reconstruction in the church: *How do we know if we are winning?*

How do we know the deconstruction of racism is achieving the results we are seeking in the church? How do we measure anti-racist reconstruction and assess our movement toward the end of racism in the church? Are we there yet? Is the most crucial question for anti-racism travelers how to seek "a path toward lasting change"? Are we on the right path? How do we know when we've arrived?

In chapter 5, we identified three standards of measurement that are helpful but ultimately are incomplete—legality, opportunity, and intentionality. See page 118 in chapter 5 to review the discussion about these three measuring tools. These conclusions apply also to the church:

Racism doesn't obey the law.
Racism ignores opportunity.
Racism doesn't care about our good intentions.

The one sure way to measure the presence or absence of racism is by measuring results. As organizing teams in the church develop strategic plans with short-term and long-term goals for our congregations and judicatories, we need also to become increasingly clear about the outcomes we seek. In the early part of our journey, the very notion of a world or a church without race may be too foreign for many of us to comprehend or too overwhelming to imagine. But as we progress, with increasing understanding of what race is and why it was created, we will gain the impetus to move from the unimaginable to the imaginable. Our paralysis will turn into a hopeful vision of freedom from racism. Our vision will translate into achievable goals. And our goals will translate into clear outcomes we can believe in, pray for, and work for. What does racism want? And in response, what are the outcomes we seek?

+ Racism seeks to separate us from God our Creator and from one another.

  The outcome we seek is a restored, anti-racist family of God.

+ Racism has stolen our sacred stories and seeks to use them as tools of inhuman oppression to support racism.

  The outcome we seek is taking back our stolen sacred stories and reclaiming an anti-racist gospel.

+ Racism seeks to dominate the church with a twisted form of race-based identity, race-based history, and race-based culture.

  The outcome we seek is a church with deracialized identity, deracialized history, and deracialized culture, a church where the absence of race matters.

+ Racism seeks to thwart God's call to resist its evil power.

  The outcome we seek is to stand on the shoulders of the saints who have struggled before us.

+ Our first task is to take the message of anti-racism inside our congregations and judicatories, to become an anti-racist church.

The outcome we seek is to become a powerful, anti-racist church, taking the message of anti-racism outside to the world.

READER'S REFLECTION

What is your vision of a restructured and accountable anti-racist denomination, congregation, or religious institution? It's not too soon to dream, visualize, and plan for the day when anti-racism will be not simply a transitory desire of a few but the defined structure and design that is recognized throughout the institution.

What will your denomination, congregation, or religious institution look like with real power sharing, assured cultural inclusion, mutual accountability, diversity without disparity, and a sense of self-perpetuating restored community?

We should not underestimate the seriousness and the difficulties of the task before us. To confront racism is to confront the diabolical presence of evil. To take on this enemy within the church and society is to take on a threatening killer that will resist elimination until its very dying moment. Yet only by recognizing the presence of this enemy in ourselves, our churches, and every part of society is there a chance of overcoming this monster that will not easily be made to go away. It takes courage to stare this malicious enemy in its face. We need to pray fervently for the ability to overcome our fear of doing so. As Saint Paul has taught us, we cannot take on the power of evil without putting on the armor of God. If we are going to take on the diabolical power of racism, we need a solid rock to stand on.

The writer of the epistle to the Hebrews reminds us that we have been not only called by God to do this work but also carried on the shoulders of those who have struggled before us:

Therefore, since we are surrounded by so great a cloud of witnesses, let us also lay aside every weight and the sin that clings so closely, and let us run with perseverance the race that is set before us. (Heb 12:1)

And Saint Paul's letter to the Ephesians encourages us:

Finally, be strong in the Lord and in the strength of his power. Put on the whole armor of God, so that you may be able to stand against the wiles of the devil. For our struggle is not against enemies of blood and flesh, but against the rulers, against the authorities, against the cosmic powers of this present darkness, against the spiritual forces of evil in the heavenly places. Therefore take up the whole armor of God, so that you may be able to withstand on that evil day, and having done everything, to stand firm. (Eph 6:10–13)

The Third Reconstruction era is drawing near. Let's be ready for it!

BIBLIOGRAPHY

Books

Alexander, Michelle. *The New Jim Crow: Mass Incarceration in the Age of Color-blindness*. New York: New Press, 2010.

Allen, Douglas W. *The Institutional Revolution: Measurement and the Economic Emergence of the Modern World. Chicago and London*. Chicago: University of Chicago Press, 2012.

Ashley, Willard W. C. *New Rules for Radicals: TNT (Techniques and Tactics) for Faith-Based Leaders*. Valley Forge, PA: Judson, 2021.

Barber, William J. *The Third Reconstruction: How a Moral Movement Is Overcoming the Politics of Division and Fear*. Boston: Beacon, 2016.

Barndt, Joseph. *Becoming an Anti-racist Church: Journeying toward Wholeness*. Minneapolis: Fortress, 2011.

———. *Understanding and Dismantling Racism: The Twenty-First Century Challenge to White America*. Minneapolis: Fortress, 2007.

Battalora, Jacqueline. *The Invention of White People and Its Relevance Today*. Houston: Strategic, 2013.

Bennett, Lerone. *Before the Mayflower: A History of Black America*. 25th anniversary ed. New York: Penguin, 1961.

Billings, David. *Deep Denial: The Persistence of White Supremacy in United States History and Life*. Roselle, NJ: Crandall, Dostie & Douglass, 2016.

Bonilla-Silva, Eduardo. *Racism without Racists: Color-Blind Racism and the Persistence of Racial Inequality in the U.S*. Lanham, MD: Rowman & Littlefield, 2003.

———. *White Supremacy and Racism in the Post–Civil Rights Era*. London: Lynne Rienner, 2001.

Bowser, Benjamin P., and Raymond G. Hunt. *Impacts of Racism on White Americans*. 2nd ed. Newbury Park, CA: Sage, 1996.

Branch, Taylor. *Parting the Waters: America in the King Years 1954–63*. New York: Simon & Schuster, 1988.

Braxton, Brad R. *No Longer Slaves: Galatians and African American Experience.* Collegeville, MN: Liturgical, 2002.

Chisom, Ronald, and Michael Washington. *Undoing Racism: A Philosophy of International Social Change.* Chicago: People's Institute Press, 1997.

Coates, Ta-Nehisi. *Between the World and Me.* New York: Spiegel & Grau, 2015.

Cone, James H. *God of the Oppressed.* Maryknoll, NY: Orbis, 1997.

Cushing, Bonnie, ed. *Accountability and White Anti-racist Organizing: Stories from Our Work.* Roselle, NJ: Crandall, Dostie & Douglass, 2010.

Deloria, Vine. *God Is Red: A Native View of Religion.* Golden, CO: Fulcrum, 1994.

Du Bois, W. E. B. *The Souls of Black Folk.* Reprint, New York: Penguin, 1989.

Emerson, Michael O., and Christian Smith. *Divided by Faith: Evangelical Religion and the Problem of Race in America.* New York: Oxford University Press, 2000.

Feagin, Joe. *Systemic Racism.* New York: Routledge, 2006.

Felder, Cain Hope. *Churches and the Black Freedom Movement, 1950–1970.* New York: Oxford University Press, 1989.

———. *Race, Racism, and the Biblical Narratives.* Minneapolis: Fortress, 2002.

Findlay, James F., Jr. *Church People in the Struggle: The National Council of Churches and the Black Freedom Movement, 1950–1970.* New York: Oxford University Press, 1993.

Franklin, John Hope. *From Slavery to Freedom: A History of African Americans.* New York: Knopf, 1994.

Freire, Paulo. *Pedagogy of the Oppressed.* New York: Herder & Herder, 1970.

Haney-López, Ian F. *White by Law: The Legal Construction of Race.* New York: New York University Press, 1996.

Harding, Vincent. *There Is a River: The Black Struggle for Freedom in America.* New York: Vintage, 1983.

Higginbotham, Leon A., Jr. *In the Matter of Color: Race and the American Legal Process: The Colonial Period.* New York: Oxford University Press, 1980.

———. *Race, Racism, and the Biblical Narratives.* Minneapolis: Fortress, 2002.

Kendi, Ibram X. *How to Be an Antiracist.* New York: Penguin Random House, 2019.

Lincoln, C. Eric. *Race, Religion, and the Continuing American Dilemma.* New York: Hill & Wang, 1984.

Marzouk, Safwat. *Intercultural Church: A Biblical Vision in an Age of Migration.* Minneapolis: Fortress, 2019.

Matthews, Michael-Ray, Marie Clare P. Onwubuariri, Cody J. Sanders, eds. *Trouble the Water: A Christian Resource for the Work of Racial Justice.* Macon, GA: Nurturing Faith, 2017.

Okun, Tema. *The Emperor Has No Clothes: Teaching Race and Racism to People Who Don't Want to Know.* Charlotte, NC: Information Age, 2010.

Rodríguez, Victor M. *Latino Politics in the United States: Race, Ethnicity, Class and Gender in the Mexican American and Puerto Rican Experience.* Dubuque, IA: Kendall Hunt, 2005.

Roediger, David. *Towards the Abolition of Whiteness: Essays on Race, Politics, and Working Class History.* New York: Verso, 1994.

Smedley, Audrey. *Race in North America: Origin and Evolution of a Worldview.* Boulder, CO: Westview, 1999.

Stevenson, Brian. *Just Mercy: A Story of Justice and Redemption.* New York: Spiegel & Grau, 2014.

Takaki, Ronald. *A Different Mirror: A History of Multicultural America.* New York: Little, Brown, 1993.

Tatum, Beverly Daniel. *Why Are All the Black Kids Sitting Together in the Cafeteria?* New York: Basic Books, 1997.

Tinker, George E. *Spirit and Resistance: Political Theology and American Indian Liberation.* Minneapolis: Fortress, 2004.

Tise, Larry E. *Proslavery: A History of the Defense of Slavery in America, 1701–1840.* Athens: University of Georgia Press, 1987.

Williams, Reggie L. *Bonhoeffer's Black Jesus: Harlem Renaissance Theology and an Ethic of Resistance.* Waco, TX: Baylor University Press, 2021.

Wink, Walter. *Naming the Powers: The Language of Power in the New Testament.* Philadelphia: Fortress, 1984.

Zinn, Howard. *A People's History of the United States: 1492 to Present.* New York: HarperCollins, 2003.

Videos

Blackside Production Company. *Eyes on the Prize.* Description by Kenneth Chisholm on IMDb. Released January 21, 1987. Created by Henry

Hampton. Featuring Julian Bond, Coretta Scott King, and Andrew Young. https://www.imdb.com/title/tt0092999/?ref_=ttpl_pl_tt.

This is a documentary series about the glory years of the American civil rights movement, starting in 1955 with the murder of Emmett Till and the subsequent trial and ending with the civil rights march to Selma in 1965. Along the way, the series touches on the major figures of the movement, such as Martin Luther King and Rosa Parks, and major incidents, such as the Little Rock school riots and the Montgomery, Alabama, transit boycott.

California Newsreel. *RACE: The Power of an Illusion*. Description by Harvard Library Diversity, Inclusion, and Belonging Collection. Released 2003. Directed by Llewellyn M. Smith, Tracy Heather Strain, and Christine Herbes-Sommers. Produced by Larry Adelman. https://projects.iq.harvard.edu/hksdigitalbookdisplay/publications/race-power-illusion.

[This] is a three-part documentary series produced by California Newsreel that investigates the idea of race in society, science and history. The educational documentary originally screened on American public television and was primarily funded by the Corporation for Public Broadcasting, the Ford Foundation and PBS.

PBS Documentaries. *The Black Church: This Is Our Story. This Is Our Song*. Description on PBS.org. Released February 16, 2021. Directed by Stacey L. Holman, Shayla Harris, and Christopher Bryson. Featuring Henry Louis Gates Jr. https://www.pbs.org/weta/black-church/.

[This] a moving four-hour, two-part series from executive producer, host and writer Henry Louis Gates, Jr., the Alphonse Fletcher University Professor at Harvard University and director of the Hutchins Center for African and African American Research, that traces the 400-year-old story of the Black church in America, all the way down to its bedrock role as the site of African American survival and grace, organizing and resilience, thriving and testifying, autonomy and freedom, solidarity and speaking truth to power.

The documentary reveals how Black people have worshipped and, through their spiritual journeys, improvised ways to bring their faith traditions from Africa to the New World, while translating them into a form of Christianity that was not only truly their own, but a redemptive force for a nation whose original sin was found in their ancestors' enslavement across the Middle Passage.

A production of McGee Media, Inkwell Media and WETA Washington, D.C., in association with Get Lifted.